Front-Line Kent

Defence against invasion from
1500 to the Cold War

Victor Smith

Maidstone 2003

Foreword

Kent has always been in the front-line of the defence of Britain, certainly from Roman times onwards. The White Cliffs of Dover, with the majestic medieval and later castle warning off intruders from on high, have become symbolic of a nation's determination to safeguard its freedom. But there is much more. Spread around the coast and inland there is a wealth of sites which tell the tale, not only of Kent and England's struggles over the centuries with the world beyond, but also of the development of technology as applied to military architecture. It is a story of thrust and counter-thrust, with the need for new defensive measures to respond to innovations in attack. Some of this story and some of the associated sites are well known but other aspects are more elusive with the related physical remains buried or hidden from view.

Recent years have seen a recognition that military architecture, while not always beautiful, is an important heritage asset, which, for all its physical presence, is vulnerable to the ravages of time. It is a resource for education, for tourism and for leisure.

Between 1999 and 2001 Kent County Council has been co-ordinating an Historic Fortifications Network with partners in Nord-Pas de Calais and West Flanders as part of an Interreg IIA programme to develop the historic fortifications of the region as a tourism product. In Kent the project has involved English Heritage, the Medway Authority and the districts of Canterbury, Dover and Shepway. New interpretation has been provided at key sites and more generally through guides and leaflets, but it has also been important to take stock of Kent's military architecture as an historic asset. What exactly do we have? What are the conservation needs? What potential does it have for education and tourism? Detailed studies have been carried out by English Heritage on a number of Kent's fortifications, including Dover Western Heights, and Victor Smith and Andrew Saunders, another leading expert in the history of military architecture, have undertaken a strategic overview of the resource.

In this volume, Victor Smith, drawing on the vast range of knowledge which he has accumulated over many years, gives us a new and fascinating account of Front- Line Kent from the time of Henry VIII to the present day. It is a story of how changing situations have required new responses. Much of the story is all around us in the towns and countryside of Kent and a gazetteer is provided to help us find both the well-known and the more elusive sites. Hopefully we will all get a better appreciation of a key part of Kent's history!

Sarah Hohler
Deputy Leader and Cabinet Member for Strategic Planning
Kent County Council

John Williams
Head of Heritage Conservation
Kent County Council

Contents

'Winnie', one of the giant long-range guns near Dover
Imperial War Museum

Introduction

'The Channel is but a ditch and anyone may cross it who has the courage.' Napoleon Bonaparte's confident assertion of 1803 mirrored a long-standing concern in Britain about the vulnerability of its coasts to invasion via the short sea crossing from France. That is why maintaining British naval superiority has always been so important: it provided a first line of defence. But, if the fleet were to be defeated or evaded, then the defences along the coast and in its hinterland would become the all-important 'front line'. As the closest part of Britain to mainland Europe, Kent has always been at the forefront of precautions against raid or invasion.

  This book covers Kent's defences during the distinctive period from the beginning of the Age of Gunpowder in the fourteenth century to the era of potential megadeath during the Cold War. It explains where and when these defences were built and why – as a response both to international tensions and fear of invasion and to the threats and opportunities opened up by emerging military technology. It reveals and discusses the physical remains (in stone, brick, earth, concrete and steel) of an era when Britain and her continental neighbours settled their differences by force of arms.

The Roman fort at Richborough
Kent County Council

Dover Castle
Kent County Council

View in the 1860s of the forts guarding the entrance to the Medway: Garrison Point Fort (left) and the defences of Grain, including Grain Tower (right)

Illustrated London News

Most developments in the science of fortification and defence are represented in the county, through a remarkable diversity of forts, batteries and other types of structures surviving from various periods. And across the Channel there are both similar and contrasting defences along the French coast.

Beginnings

Defensive structures have existed in Kent since the pre-Roman tribal hill forts, of which examples exist at Bigbury and Oldbury. The first system of organised coastal defence was during the Roman occupation, when forts were built from the Wash to the Solent, and the Roman fleet patrolled the seas. In Kent there are standing remains of the forts at Reculver, Richborough and Lympne and part of the bastion of a fort at Dover.

The Saxon era has left no obvious defensive signature in Kent, but with the Norman Conquest came extensive castle-building. Castles were used as a means to establish and maintain control of territory and as an instrument of government – and, in coastal areas, as a local defence against raiders. Initially they were built in earth and timber (there is a fine example at Castle Hill at Folkestone). Then stone structures appeared, the most striking of which are the castles at Dover, Rochester, Canterbury, Tonbridge and Eynsford. In medieval England domestic insecurity caused as much anxiety as the fear of foreign invasion, but from the later fifteenth century internal stability improved, and defence against invasion became the greater concern.

In the fifteenth and sixteenth centuries (until Calais was lost in 1558) England's strategic problems were complicated by her having to protect her territory on the Channel coast of France and, thereafter, to defend the offshore remains of that territory: the Channel Islands. Added to this was the need to secure Ireland. In 1603 the Union of the English and Scottish Crowns removed the need to guard a land frontier with Scotland, although there were Jacobite rebellions in 1715 and 1745. It was only during the

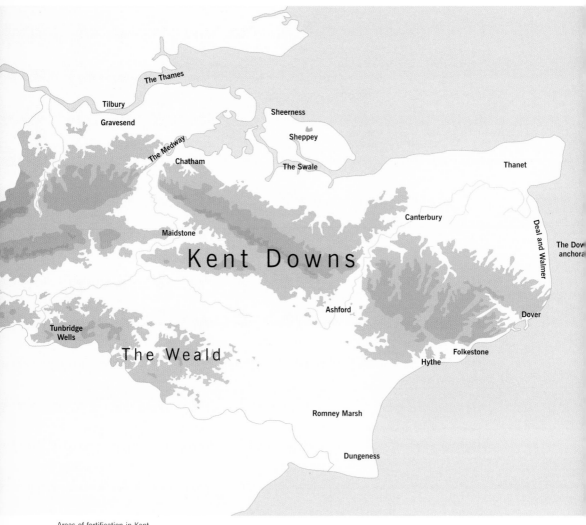

The Thames

Tilbury

Gravesend

Sheerness

Sheppey

The Medway

Chatham

The Swale

Thanet

Canterbury

Maidstone

Kent Downs

Deal and Walmer

The Dow anchora

Ashford

Dover

Tunbridge
Wells

The Weald

Folkestone

Hythe

Romney Marsh

Dungeness

Areas of fortification in Kent

Tonbridge Castle
Kent County Council

Rochester Castle keep
Kent County Council

English Civil Wars of the 1640s that, for a time, internal insecurity seriously revived. Subsequently, the acquisition of a growing colonial empire added a world-wide dimension to British strategic planning.

Until the twentieth century, the external threat to Britain was exclusively seaborne, so the need was to provide coastal defences for harbours and landing beaches. Fortified estuaries and anchorages in Kent such as the Thames, the Medway, Dover and the Downs also provided secure bases both for the British fleet and for the dispatch of expeditionary forces. Whereas Britain's only frontier was her coast, continental states like France needed to defend not only their coastlines but land borders as well. This led to a different strategic pattern of fortifications on the continent, with zones of fortified towns, castles and forts created to guard against the threat of armies crossing land frontiers. Nord-Pas de Calais was an important strategic element of the French north-east land frontier (as its surviving fortifications testify). As in Britain, though, continental fortifications did not exist in isolation but were part of a wider military organisation.

Geographical factors

Geography limited the points on the Kentish coast where an invader could land. It also influenced the location of harbours and naval and military centres that an invader might need to blockade to prevent the forces they contained being used against him. Terrain helped determine the positions to be adopted for defence, whether on the coast or inland. High cliffs or marshland, on the one hand, or flat dry ground, on the other, offered difficulties or opportunities for a landing; rivers, valleys, roads and hills suggested ways for an invader to penetrate inland and also holding positions for a defender. The North Downs, in particular, were well situated for defenders, especially where they run close to London – whose capture would have been an invader's primary objective.

The defiant chalk cliffs along the coast between Folkestone and Kingsdown were a formidable and symbolic natural obstacle to seaborne landings, but in the middle of them was the Dour Gap, and there lay Dover harbour, from which roads led inland. To capture Dover and then use it as a port of resupply was vital to an invading army, so this 'key to England', was nationally important and heavily defended. Further west, Folkestone harbour was smaller, but it too had road access inland, and there was another possible landing place for an enemy at Hythe. Beyond that, the coastline fronting Romney Marsh and Dungeness had landing beaches, as well as extensive offshore anchorages.

North of Kingsdown, the Walmer–Sandown coast had long been recognised as a landing beach; offshore was the important Downs anchorage, sheltered by the Goodwin Sands, which an invasion fleet might use. The coastline along to Sandwich also offered landing opportunities and, further on, Thanet's small bays and harbours were suitable for limited landing operations or raids. Thereafter, the north Kent coast between Thanet and the Swale lacked any suitable harbours and was unattractive for a landing of any size. West of the Swale, areas of marsh fringing the Thames and Medway presented difficulties to an enemy intending to land a large force.

The Thames was, however, a vulnerable route to the capital, and an anchorage for much mercantile shipping; from the sixteenth century it was also the site of two royal dockyards and, later, the arsenal and magazines at Woolwich and Purfleet. Defence of the Thames was therefore vital to the security of the nation. On the lower reaches of the Medway, the evolution of the dockyards at Chatham from the sixteenth century and at Sheerness from the seventeenth, together with the use of the river as a naval anchorage, made it a tempting target for a raid. Moreover, the bridge over the Medway at Rochester carried the strategically important main road between London and the Kent coast, the use of which would have been vital to an invader landing in the county. Roads in Kent improved in number and quality from the later eighteenth century, and in the nineteenth century railways were added. These routes provided an improved infrastructure for deploying defending forces (though they could also be useful to an invader, once he had made his landing).

Any invasion would thus involve the Walmer–Sandown and Folkestone–Romney Marsh coastlines as the most likely landing points, with the probability of attacks on Dover, the Thames and Medway and perhaps Thanet. These geographical constraints on an invader remained until World War II, by which time enemy forces could also be landed from the air at any of a number of places behind the coastline.

The White Cliffs at Dover
Kent County Council

The technological dimension

The emergence of gunpowder artillery from the fourteenth century was to have a profound effect on warfare and defensive methods, and by the early sixteenth century artillery had become an effective weapon. However, over the next two-and-a-half centuries its progress was gradual.

From the late eighteenth century the acceleration of technical progress that we call the Industrial Revolution intensified the contest between offence and defence and artillery improved in range, accuracy and destructive power. This process gathered pace by the fourth decade of the nineteenth century, and soon evolved into a long-running competition between states to achieve parity or superiority in weapon systems. From the later 1850s this was exemplified in the emergence of the steam-powered ironclad warship, armed with rifled guns, and in the British defences built in the 1860s to counter them. The introduction of long-range breech-loading guns, magazine rifles and machine-guns later in the nineteenth century also had a fundamental effect, with many of the earlier defensive structures being superseded and new ones built. In parallel with this a more decentralised approach to the defence of land fronts evolved: one which more than ever emphasised the skilful use of firepower itself, rather than the structures in which it was located. These trends resulted in fewer

New technology: heavy rifled muzzle-loading guns at Woolwich Arsenal in 1874
Illustrated London News

Armoured warfare: production lines for British tanks at Cowley during WW2

guns being mounted on fortifications and ships than in the smooth-bore age.

By the second decade of the twentieth century, the prospect of bombing attack from the air began to add a threatening new dimension. During World War I a new strategy for defence was developed to deal with this, involving the use of fighter interceptors and anti-aircraft guns, but in World War II air power became a still more devastating threat. Civil defence was provided, and radar detection – which adapted electronics and radio to give dramatically improved early warning of air attack – made the use of air-defence fighters and anti-aircraft guns more effective. Utilising these technical advances, guns and fighter aircraft could provide some defence against attack by V1 pulsejet-powered flying bombs, although there was no defence against V2 ballistic missiles arriving at 3,000 mph. Meanwhile, motor propelled weapons, including tanks, had already been used in World War I and by World War II their use had become an integral part of military strategy. They brought with them the likelihood of bold thrusts across the country in the event of an invasion – in addition to paratroop and glider-borne landings – and protection against them required defensive innovation and a move to inland networks of defence.

During the Cold War the main risk was of a nuclear holocaust, and also the possible use of biological or chemical weapons in an attack. By the 1960s home defence had come to rely more upon air-defence systems elsewhere in Britain and on the continent and upon the deterrent effect of nuclear weapons deployed elsewhere in the NATO alliance (including those in submarines). The construction of command and control bunkers in Kent was a feature of this period.

By the twentieth century, methods of defence had changed dramatically since the start of the gunpowder era. Structures from each stage of this long period of evolution may be seen in Kent. The continued survival of, and access to, these heritage assets enriches our understanding and enjoyment of history and of our cultural heritage.

Castles and Cannon

1

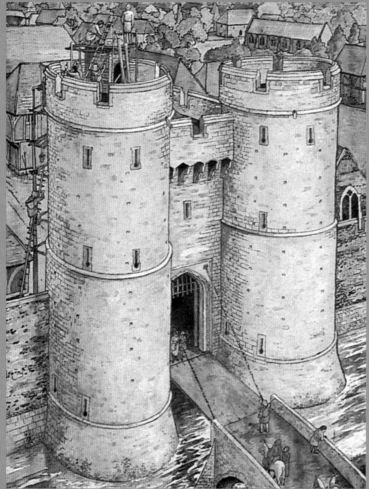

Artist's impression of Canterbury Westgate in about 1400
Canterbury Archaeological Trust, artist Laurie Sartin

The introduction of gunpowder artillery
from the fourteenth century was to change
the nature of warfare on land and at sea.
Among the most enduringly visible features
of this process were changes in the design
and use of fortifications, of which fine
examples may be seen in Kent.

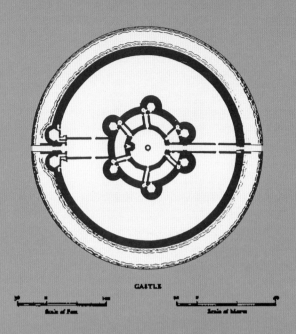

CASTLE

Scale of Feet   Scale of Metres

Queenborough Castle from an Elizabethan plan
HMSO

The introduction of firearms

Gunpowder firearms appeared in Europe by no later than the 1320s. Early English illustrations of them show crude, flask-like objects for firing arrows, although roundshot were known at this date. Other guns were made of iron tubes with bands shrunk over them to withstand the pressures from the explosion of a gunpowder charge.

To begin with, these new weapons were of limited effectiveness (although the loud noise of their firing could frighten horses and discomfort soldiers) and slow to influence either tactics or the design of fortifications. Nonetheless, they were increasingly used in battle, and, as their effectiveness improved, the potential of firearms became apparent. Larger guns were made, capable of being used, along with the older, torsion-powered siege engines, to batter the walls of castles and towns.

A process of adaptation

In England, as on the continent, the designers of fortifications responded cautiously to the new weapons, continuing with the medieval tradition of high stone walls and towers but adapting them to include small gun loops. Sometimes these were circular, occasionally in the shape of a bar-bell, but more often keyhole-shaped gun loops were used, a modification of the earlier arrow slit. From these small apertures hand weapons could be fired, though with a limited field of fire, so that multiple loops were necessary to cover the ground in front of the walls. Firearms were still one element in a mix of close-defence weapons that included longbows and crossbows, lances and swords (indeed, at this period the longbow was a more accurate weapon and had a higher rate of fire than a handgun). They could be used from any suitable aperture or embrasure in, or on, walls, towers and gates. Heavier counter-siege weapons might also be mounted by adapting existing structures or by mounting them in new earthen positions called bulwarks.

French raids lead to improved defences

Between 1337 and 1453, during the rather intermittent 'Hundred Years' War', England and France were in conflict over the English-owned domains in France, and Edward III even laid claim to the French throne. Especially in the later fourteenth century, the adaptation of defences in Kent to the use of firearms coincided with a period of French attacks on English shipping in the Channel and in river estuaries, and raids along the south coast, from Devon to Essex. In Kent, Gravesend and Sandwich were burnt in 1380 and 1400 respectively.

The frequency of the raiding provoked both royal concern and local anxiety. As a result, the Crown repaired and strengthened the castles for which it was responsible and encouraged local magnates and townships to provide better protection for themselves. The latter required Royal grants of crenellation (to permit the building of fortifications) and of murage (authority to levy local taxes to help finance construction).

As part of the upgrading process in Kent, the circular and innovative Queenborough Castle (1361–77) was provided with gunpowder artillery as well as catapults; its walls are no longer visible, but the site can be seen as a low grassed mound. In the 1380s the castles at Cooling, Saltwood and Dover, as well as Canterbury's Westgate and town walls were equipped with firearms, and gun loops may be seen at all these sites (those at Hever Castle, too, may date from this period). Canterbury is important as an extensive surviving example of the adaptation of the fortified circuit of a town to defence with firearms. The now vanished town walls of Dover were probably similarly protected, and the walls of Rochester, a town on a river with direct access from the Thames Estuary, may well have been given additional protection during this time of anxiety.

Along the French Channel coast, town walls and castles were similarly being adapted for the use of firearms; at Bergues, for instance, circular loops were provided in the 1420s, and there were new works at Calais and, later, at Montreuil. Inland, the towers of Ypres were given gun loops in the 1390s.

Outer gateway of Cooling Castle
Kent County Council

The inner ward of Cooling Castle
Kent County Council

Gun loop in tower of Canterbury town wall
Canterbury City Council

Guns at the English siege of Rouen in 1419
Bibliothèque Nationale, Paris

Gun loops at Canterbury Westgate
Simon Curtis

To warn of an impending attack, a network of fire beacons was established along and behind the south coast of England. These were lit by observers when an enemy was spotted, so that defensive forces could be mobilised. The Cinque Ports had traditionally provided naval defence of a kind, in the form of an obligation to provide ship service to the Crown, as much for transporting English troops to fight in France as for protection against French raiding. But this institution was starting to decline during the later fourteenth century and royal ships began to form the core of the fleet. The earliest known list of royal ships dates from 1417.

The French raiding continued. Sandwich, whose early fortifications are well defined, was attacked again in 1438 and its defences were strengthened. By 1451 an artillery bulwark had been added at the south-east of the town, and this was troublesome to the French when they attacked yet again in 1457 (but their attack still succeeded, and they burnt the town). That bulwark was reinstated and another one, built in brick, added near Fishergate. The brick-built Herstmonceux Castle in Sussex was erected in 1440 – a specimen of late medieval monumentalism and martial display, its gun ports belied by the presence of large windows – and in 1456–7 an artillery position was added to Rye's defences.

From the middle of the fifteenth century the range and penetrative ability of artillery improved. The breaching of Constantinople's defences by Turkish guns in 1453 showed that even strong town walls were at risk against artillery. More influential was the way in which French artillery had been used to batter the walls and compel the surrender of a succession of castles and towns during the Charles VIII's invasion of the Italian peninsula in 1494 – moreover, that campaign had demonstrated that powerful artillery was becoming more mobile. Land warfare was endemic

The use of artillery during a medieval siege
British Library

on the continent, making it imperative for states to rethink their approach
to defence and the design of fortifications. This resulted in the use in
fortifications of earth and substantially thickened walls so as to withstand
the shock of artillery bombardment, bastions and towers with rounded
forms to help deflect shot, and the provision of more purpose-built
positions and larger gun ports for artillery powerful enough to counter
that of a besieger. On the continent, this is again shown in the town
defences along the French Channel coast: at Bergues, where new gun
ports date from the end of the fifteenth century or the early sixteenth,
at Boulogne and at Gravelines (whose castle was rebuilt by Charles V
between 1528 and 1536). However, it was engineers in the Italian states
who showed the most innovative thinking in the early sixteenth century,
developing striking new designs built around the use of the gun.

  Before the sixteenth century opened, the days of the castle as an integral
part of England's defences were nearly over. It was a badge of feudalism,
part of a politico-social structure that had almost disappeared. Despite
the internal turmoil of the fifteenth century, government in England
was becoming increasingly centralised, and, except as a royal or private
residence, the castle no longer had an important place in the political
structure of the country. Moreover, it had become vulnerable to the power
of gunpowder artillery. New approaches had therefore to be developed.
Defence had to be assigned a place as an institution of the centralised
state, rather than as a function exercised through feudal vassals, and the
form of defensive structures on the ground had to change to meet the
evolving technology and tactics of artillery.

Deal Castle, Chris Peyer©

Henry VIII's
New Fortifications

Castles
Blockhouses

2

Possible 16th century bulwark in
the western moat of Dover Castle
James Chapelard

Artillery was increasingly being used on warships at sea, and this was a new factor to be considered by those responsible for the design of coastal defences. From the early sixteenth century improvements enabled land-based guns to fight a stand-off action with enemy ships at long range, so as to protect a harbour, anchorage or a landing place. This was demonstrated in Henry VIII's extensive programme of defence construction, which has left impressive survivals on the Kent coast. This marked the beginning of a long competition for superiority between seaborne and land-based artillery.

Purpose-built artillery defences had already appeared in England during the reign of Henry VII, a notable example being Dartmouth Castle in Devon (1480s). In Kent, two circular masonry towers with gun ports and embrasures were built to protect Dover's new harbour (formed 1500–20). These were soon lost to the sea, but near Rye, in Sussex, a tower (1512–14) of similar form still survives; it formed the core of the later Camber Castle. On the continent, the English built a circular tower at Tournai.

A deteriorating relationship between England and her continental neighbours followed Henry VIII's break with the Roman Church in 1533. The situation worsened by 1538, when the rivalry between France and the Habsburg Empire for the domination of Europe (which Henry had been able to manipulate by backing one side against the other) was replaced by a Franco-Habsburg truce. This left England politically isolated, and the Pope encouraged other states to invade and restore the country to the authority of the Roman See. The English response was to mobilise the fleet, muster the militia and to appoint commissioners to make proposals for the defence of the English coast and the English possessions in France.

It was unrealistic to attempt to defend the entire English coastline, so efforts concentrated on securing the more important anchorages, harbours and landing grounds along the coast from Hull to Milford Haven. The new structures were exclusively Royal and military. A central design office was set up to help carry forward this programme, and efforts were also made to develop a more powerful domestic armament industry, both to fulfil the new demand for land-based and seaborne guns and to reduce reliance on purchases from abroad.

Most of the new English fortifications employed designs with low, rounded bastions, their guns mounted on two- or four-wheeled carriages in enclosed rooms, called casemates, and firing through purpose-designed ports. Other guns fired through roof-top embrasures in parapets that were sloping or rounded to deflect incoming shot. The influence on design was North European – probably derived from a variety of sources, including advice from foreign specialists such as the Moravian military engineer Stephan von Haschenperg, the recent military experience and architectual knowledge of others involved in planning the defences and, perhaps, Albrecht Dürer's Treatise on Fortification (Nuremberg, 1527), which portrayed many of the features present in the new English defences. Henry himself also contributed significantly to the designs.

A deteriorating relationship between England and her continental neighbours followed Henry VIII's break with the Roman Church in 1533.

Durer's proposal for a bastion with casemates and smoke vents and curved parapet

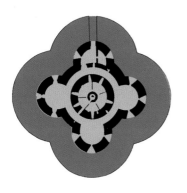 

Plans of Walmer Castle (left),
Sandgate Castle (centre) and
Deal Castle (right)
HMSO

Castles

More defences were built in Kent than in any other county, with works
constructed at Dover, on the Deal coast, at Sandgate and in the Thames
estuary. The plans of the 'castles' at Walmer, Deal and Sandown, symbolic
of Henry's defiance and exemplars of the new approach, have been likened
to the form of a Tudor Rose (though this was purely coincidental). The
largest and most elaborate was Deal, which projects a solid grandeur. A
central circular tower rises above six small attached rounded bastions,
separated from an outer ring of six larger bastions by a courtyard. The
main armament fired through embrasures on the top of the tower and
bastions and through a pair of gun ports either side of the entrance.
Loopholes for small arms such as the 'hackbus' or 'arquebus' were
incorporated in the walls of both inner and outer bastions (in the latter
case to defend the ditch), and living accommodation and magazines were
provided within the bastions. Walmer and Sandown were simpler, having
both gun ports and embrasures but just one level of four bastions around
their central towers. Although principally intended to fire to seaward, the
forts were individually capable of all-round fire. With now vanished earthen
batteries and trenches between the castles, this complex of fortifications
covered a stretch of water and beach some 4 miles (6.3 km) long, although
only a small proportion of the guns was powerful enough to seriously
damage a warship. Deal and Walmer are both open to visitors, but nothing
is visible of Sandown (a casualty of coastal erosion and the building of sea

Gun ports of Walmer Castle
Victor Smith

Walmer Castle
Channel Photography

View of Sandgate Castle
Kent County Council

defences), although a plaque marks the spot. On the cliff-top at Kingsgate is an 18th century folly, apparently built in imitation of Walmer and Sandown Castles.

Dover's new defences were outside the mainstream of contemporary fortification design. Consisting of three unsophisticated earth-and-timber batteries or bulwarks; two were sited below the castle cliffs and a third a little further west at Archcliffe. Their purpose was to defend the approaches to the harbour and the beach between the town and the castle. In 1544, a fourth bulwark was added on the outer King's Pier. None now remain (although the site of one under the castle became the later Mote's Bulwark). A small bulwark in the castle ditch may also date from this period. The bulwark at Archcliffe was later rebuilt as Archcliffe Fort.

Von Haschenperg was responsible for the design of Sandgate Castle, which was sited to defend the coastal road where it began to rise over the hills north-east to Dover, as well as the adjoining beach. This was a stone structure with a central circular gun tower surrounded by a triangle of three circular bastions linked by an outwardly curving curtain wall. A matching outer wall has a defensible gatehouse to landward. The inner and outer structures are pierced by a variety of gun ports and loops for small-arms, and the roofs of the inner structure had positions for guns to fire through embrasures. (The castle as it now exists reflects alterations made during the Napoleonic Wars.)

Deal Castle
English Heritage

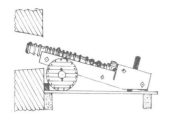

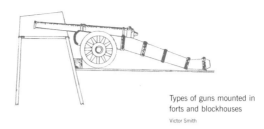

Types of guns mounted in
forts and blockhouses
Victor Smith

Blockhouses

The Thames defences protected the approaches to London and the dockyards
at Deptford and Woolwich. They consisted of five shoreline blockhouses in
two groups at either end of Gravesend Reach, three at the upper or western
end and two at the lower or eastern end. They were designed by Sir
Christopher Morris, Master of the Ordnance, and James Nedeham, Surveyor
of the King's Works, who had both served with the English army in France.
The interlocking fields of fire of the guns on opposite banks of the river
crossed the channel that enemy warships needed to take in order to sail
upstream. The upper blockhouses also guarded the Gravesend–Tilbury ferry
crossing; two of these, whose design is known, the Gravesend and Tilbury
Blockhouses, were D-shaped brick-and-masonry towers with gun ports, roof
embrasures and earthen ramparts for guns outside on the river bank. The
only portion of these defences still visible is the remnant of the brick main
structure of the Gravesend Blockhouse, which stands in front of the
Clarendon Royal Hotel on Gravesend's riverside.

The Medway was not included in the general scheme of defence building of
1539–40. The risk, however, suggested by French raiding of the south coast in
1545–7 and the need to protect the fleet anchorage that was evolving in the
Medway led to the construction of a blockhouse at Sheerness and two others
'within the Isles of Sheppey and Grain'. Queenborough Castle on Sheppey
was also adapted to take artillery. None of these works has left visible traces.

While Henry's fortifications in England were under construction in 1540,
artillery defences were also being built to defend English territory based on
Calais. Not far away, other defences were built by Francis I of France at
Montreuil (1537–49). Henry's military endeavours to hold and expand his
territory on the coast of France had given the English valuable experience
in using artillery in siege warfare but, together with the cost of the
new fortifications in England, had exhausted the Treasury's funds.

The Gravesend Blockhouse
Victor Smith

A 17th century view of
The Gravesend Blockhouse
British Library

Angular Bastions and the Spanish Armada

Angular bastions
The Spanish Armada

3

The rounded form of bastion used in Henry VIII's defences was rapidly superseded by the angular bastion system. This was to dominate military engineering in Europe and its colonies for more than 250 years. In Kent, though, it appeared at only two sites before the end of the 16th century.

Angular bastions

By the mid-1540s a new system of fortification, originating in Italy, was gradually influencing developments in northern Europe. It was based on the use of pointed, angular bastions. If applied at suitable intervals around a defensive circuit these features allowed the defenders' fire to cover all the ground in front a fortification – unlike the earlier rounded bastion, which was weakened by the presence of 'dead' ground immediately to its front.

On the continent the angular bastion became a characteristic of the perimeter fortifications of towns. Had Henry VIII's main defensive scheme of 1540 begun just a few years later, it might well have incorporated this new form. During the mid-1540s angular bastions featured in new English fortifications on the coast of France; in England these devices were incorporated at Southsea Castle (1544) near Portsmouth, and at Sandown (1545), Sharpenode (1545-7) and Yarmouth (1547) Castles, all on the Isle of Wight, as well as being built by English engineers in Scotland (1548). In Kent, a single angular bastion has been found in archaeological excavations at the rear of the Henrician blockhouse at Milton-next Gravesend (surface-marked for visitors), an addition which may date from 1545–7. The man who designed this, was perhaps Sir Richard Lee, who built an identical, and surviving bastion on the front of Upnor Castle (1559), projecting into the River Medway to defend the fleet moorings. But these were isolated uses of this defensive form.

The building of Upnor Castle had probably been spurred by a sense of insecurity and threat arising from the loss of Calais to the French in 1558, the year of Elizabeth I's accession to the throne. Elizabeth's defensive policy concentrated upon expanding the fleet, and Upnor Castle was the only new work built in southern England during the early part of her reign. Later in the century better landward defences were added, and the front block of the castle was modified. The presence of anachronistic, rounded turrets and keyhole-shaped gun ports, resulted in a structure that seems improbable for its date and is difficult to understand. At around the same time, after the French conquest of Calais, King Philip of Spain ordered the building of an angular-bastioned circuit round Gravelines, to the design of an Italian military engineer.

The façade of Upnor Castle
Kent County Council

The angular river bastion of Upnor Castle
Kent County Council

In 1574, the fleet's increasing use of the Medway led to work being started to build a bastioned fort at Swaleness to control and defend the vulnerable junction of the Swale with the Medway (this project was suspended in favour of blocking the Swale with timber piles), and angular bastioned forms featured in proposals of this date for enclosing Queenborough Castle and Sheerness with new defences. In 1579–86 Dover harbour was enlarged, enhancing its value for cross-channel communication and as a safe haven for part of the fleet.

Map of the defences of the lower Thames during the Spanish Armada in 1588
Cruden's History of Gravesend, 1843

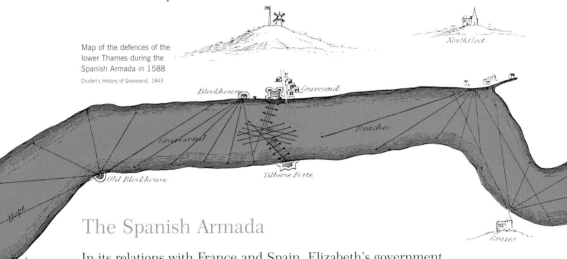

The Spanish Armada

In its relations with France and Spain, Elizabeth's government used diplomacy to prevent the direct involvement in continental wars that had been so financially ruinous for Henry VIII. However, English assistance, in 1585, to the disaffected Netherlanders seeking independence from their Spanish overlords, along with attacks on Spanish interests in the Americas and the execution of Mary, Queen of Scots in 1587, were seen as aggravating and provocative by Spain, which began preparations to invade England. This process culminated in dispatch of a flota armada (armed fleet) of 130 ships carrying 20,000 soldiers in 1588. Some 25,000 troops also waited in the Netherlands, ready to cross to England under the protection of the Spanish ships. This fleet, however, known to the British as the Spanish Armada, was defeated and scattered in the Channel, and fewer than half the Spanish ships managed to return to Spain.

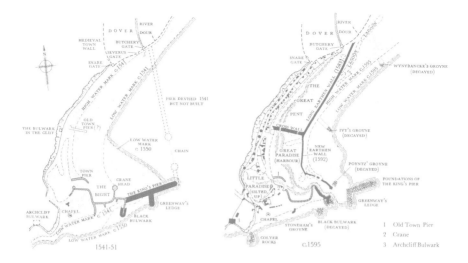

Map of Dover's harbour and defences in 1541-5 (left) and 1595 (right)
HMSO

During this crisis, many temporary fortifications were built which have left no visible traces, including boom obstacles across the Thames, the Medway and Dover harbour. The defences at these places were in varying condition at the start of the emergency and were hurriedly brought back to fighting condition. The Italian engineer Federigo Genebelli, inventor of an 'infernal machine' that blew up hundreds of Spanish troops at Antwerp, worked at Gravesend and Tilbury, where additional temporary works were made. These included an angular earthwork enclosing the land side of the Henrician Tilbury Blockhouse, traces of which may have been found in archaeological excavations. At West Tilbury, an entrenched camp was established for one of the field armies covering the land approaches to London; no definite remains of this survive, but possible cropmark traces have been seen from the air. Another military force was assembled at Dover.

  The defeat of the Spanish fleet is now seen as a landmark event in English history. The English of the time, however, drew no long-term comfort from their victory, seeing it as a breathing space, while Spain rebuilt her fleet. Indeed, there were further invasion scares in the 1590s and, in 1601 (when there was a Spanish landing in Ireland). In the decade following defeat of the Spanish Armada, new bastioned circuits were built outside Kent at Carisbrooke Castle on the Isle of Wight, at Plymouth and at Pendennis Castle in Cornwall.

Elizabethan 'Pocket Pistol' at Dover Castle
English Heritage

■ Angular Bastions and the Spanish Armada

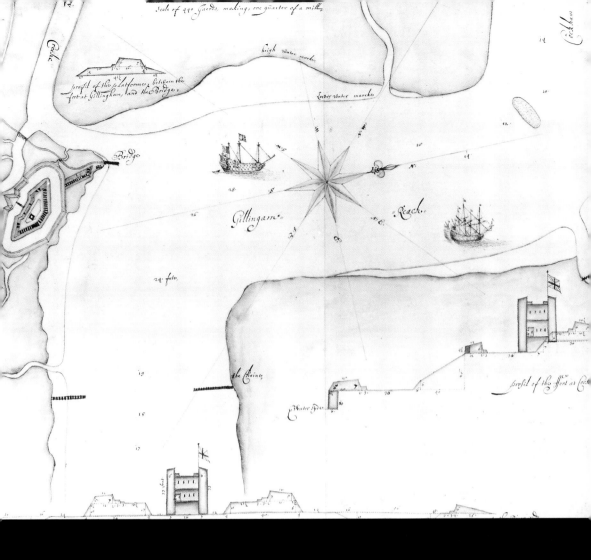

The Seventeenth Century

Peace and War
The early Stuarts
The English Civil War (1642–8)
The Dutch Raid (1667)
Bernard de Gomme and new defences

4

Peace and War

After the Treaty of London in 1604 ended the threat from Spain, the reigns of
James I (1603–25) and Charles I (1625–49) marked a period of decay for
English defences. During the English Civil War (1642–8) fortifications were
built in the war zones, and London, whose capture was a Royalist objective,
was enclosed by a large defensive circuit of forts and ramparts. Kent, though,
was in a safer position, behind the lines in Parliamentarian territory, and saw
little new construction. After the period of Cromwellian rule known as the
Commonwealth, and the eventual Restoration of the Monarchy in 1660,
tensions increased between Britain and the newly independent Netherlands,
and a Dutch raid on the Medway in 1667 helped to stimulate a burst of new
defence construction at several key places in England, notably the Medway
and the Thames estuary.

The early Stuarts

The largely inactive attitude towards
defences under the early Stuarts reflected a
greater sense of security following peace
with Spain. Moreover, the Thirty Years War
(1618–48) was seen as keeping Spain and
the other warring states embroiled in
religious strife in central Europe, too
distracted to turn their eyes across the
English Channel.

A survey of the condition of Kent's
defences in 1623 by the Office of Ordnance
shows them as in a largely fossilised state.
Three sites were listed for Dover:

Plan of Archcliffe Fort at the beginning
of the 17th century
Dover Museum

The Castle, including seaward- and
landward-facing batteries with 32 guns. Many of the gunners were
accommodated in the medieval wall towers of the castle, from which
musketry fire could be used to defend the curtain walls and ditches. The
castle's arms inventory still included longbows.

Mote's Bulwark, a small work below the castle.

Archcliffe Fort, which replaced the defences Henry VIII had built here in
the 1540s. When this fort was built is uncertain but it is shown on a plan
dated to 1604–14. Single angular bastions had been built at Milton and
Upnor in the sixteenth century, but Archcliffe was the earliest fort in Kent to
incorporate them as part of a defensive circuit: gun lines facing seaward were
joined to a curtain wall and two bastions facing the land. The landward
portion of the fort survives as rebuilt in stone in 1639–40 after a structural
collapse. Then, or shortly afterwards, a third bastion was added.

Elsewhere in Kent, the forts of the Downs were little altered. Sandown
suffered sea erosion, as did Sandgate. The survey also mentions two small

detached batteries, Baye and Warham, a short distance downstream of Upnor Castle, but no definite traces of these remain. On the Thames, the two remaining blockhouses at Gravesend and Tilbury were left untouched.

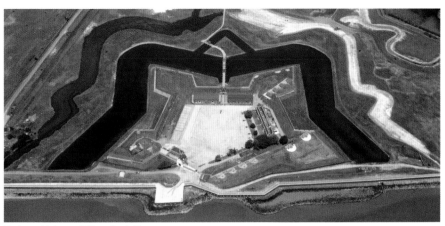

The layered defences of Tilbury Fort in Essex
Essex County Council

The English Civil War (1642–8)

Kent came under the control of Parliament at the start of the Civil War, and London and the south-east became a power-base for the Parliamentarian cause. Although much of the fleet had sided with Parliament, the Royalists succeeded in obtaining enough ships to pose a threat to the coasts. A more serious worry was that the King might obtain the help of a continental ally with a fleet and an army to recover control of England. Existing defences were therefore maintained as far as resources would allow. (For a time in 1648, the fleet and the castles of the Downs came under the control of the leaders of the short-lived royalist Kentish Rebellion.)

A map of 1756 shows a circular earthwork just north of Dover Castle, identified as 'Oliver's Mount', which may have been a Civil War outwork, and an earthwork apparently from this period was noted at Barham Down in the 1940s. Neither survive. An earthwork near Squerryes Court, Westerham, has also been suggested as a Civil War defence. In 1642–3, to guard against possible attacks by Royalist forces (which never came), London was enclosed by an 18-km-long ring of forts joined by lines. These rudimentary earthwork defences, known as the 'Lines of Communication', have left no surface traces, but parts of them have been found in archaeological excavations. (A more professional bastioned circuit protected the royalist capital at Oxford, and many other places across Britain were fortified in varying degrees, giving the country some of the characteristics of a continental war zone.)

Charles II's short-lived invasion of England from Scotland in 1651 was overcome at the Battle of Worcester on 23rd September.

The Dutch Raid (1667)

With the Commonwealth (1649–60) came new tensions. Efforts to expand trade by acquiring overseas colonies brought England into conflict with similar ambitions on the part of the Netherlands (which had finally won independence from Spain in 1648). The Navigation Acts of 1651 (which curtailed the Dutch carrying trade by specifying that all goods entering or leaving England must be moved in English ships) led to war. At the Battle of the Downs in the Channel in 1652 the English defeated the Dutch fleet. After further naval victories the war ended to the advantage of the English in 1654, but strained relations continued after the Restoration in 1660. Competition for access to the resources and commercial opportunities of overseas territories intensified, and incidents and encounters between the English and Dutch armed forces in 1664 led England to declare war the next year. By 1667 initial successes and

Dutch Ships in the Medway, June 1667 *Willem Schellinks*
© National Maritime Museum

over-optimism about the progress of the war led to much of the English fleet being decommissioned to save money, and in early June the Dutch seized the opportunity to launch an attack on the Thames and Medway. At the mouth of the Medway Admiral de Ruyter's fleet silenced a fort under construction at the new dockyard being established at Sheerness, then moved upstream, overcoming a cross-river boom and batteries at Hoo Ness and Gillingham, and entered the naval anchorage below Upnor. There it captured and removed the flagship Royal Charles and burnt six other ships. The war ended with the signing of the Treaty of Breda on July 21st but news of this was not received in England until after an indecisive naval battle, which took place at the Lower Hope of the Thames on 23rd July.

During the raid, the blockhouses at Gravesend and Tilbury were hurriedly repaired and a new temporary work, Trinity Fort, was built at Gravesend. This no longer exists.

Bernard de Gomme and new defences

The humiliation of 1667 had revealed the weakness of England's coastal defences and helped stimulate new defence construction on the Medway, the Thames and elsewhere. The Medway was vital: Chatham was now England's premier naval base, and the second dockyard being built at Sheerness was vulnerably sited at the entrance to the river.

On the continent, large systems of fortification had evolved using concentric and successive ramparts and ditches to produce defence in depth. On France's Channel coast, bastioned systems were added to the defences of Bergues, Montreuil and Dunkirk, while at Gravelines these were built by the Spanish Crown and, after their capture by Louis XIV, by French engineers. (All have left significant traces – above all at Gravelines, a key site on the French coast for viewing bastioned fortifications.)

The works at Sheerness were the largest scheme of artillery defence yet undertaken in Kent. They were designed by a master of bastioned fortification, Sir Bernard de Gomme (1620–85), the King's Chief Engineer and at the time the most accomplished military engineer in English service (he also built fortifications at Portsmouth and Plymouth). Described as an English equivalent of Vauban – the famous French military engineer of the time – this Dutch officer had acquired his competence during active service in the Netherlands' struggle for

Portrait of Sir Bernard de Gomme
British Library

independence, before taking service with Charles I in 1642. His design for the low-lying, marshy site at Sheerness reflected current Dutch practice. Built in 1668–9, the fortifications took the form of a curtain wall with terminating bastions that cut off the dockyard peninsula from the land; a ravelin fronted an entrance through the curtain wall, and an indented line with gun emplacements faced seawards. Traces of the brick and stone seaward front of the defences survive, including the remains of a base for a corner sentry box.

Sir Bernard de Gomme (1620–85), the King's Chief Engineer and at the time the most accomplished military engineer in English service

Between 1669 and the mid-1670s De Gomme built two forts further upstream, at Cockham Wood on the left bank and Gillingham on the right bank, to cover the river approaches to Chatham. Cockham Wood Fort, on the water's edge, displayed a workmanlike and pragmatic use of firepower, with guns set on two levels within a rectangular ditched enclosure; a bastion-like tower redoubt secured the rear. The outline of the fort and its ditch survives, along with the brick arches supporting the lower level of guns at the water's edge and traces of the brick tower. Gillingham Fort, (which also guarded the entrance to St Mary's Creek) was diamond-shaped and contained a square tower redoubt; guns on two faces of the diamond and in a wing battery covered the river. This fort was destroyed when Chatham dockyard was extended in the 1870s.

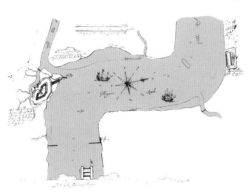

Map of the inner defences of the Medway, with Gillingham Fort (left) and Cockham Wood Fort (right)
© National Maritime Museum

De Gomme's major new work in the south-east was Tilbury Fort (1670–85), in Essex, designed to reinforce the defences of Thames. This is the best site in Britain at which to see seventeenth-century bastioned fortifications. Incorporating the earlier blockhouse, this large fort was built on a low-lying, marshy site and, with defences in depth, resembled a typical contemporary fortress in the Netherlands. Its core was a large pentagonal earthwork, revetted in red brick. Four of its corners had angular bastions pierced with gun embrasures to provide all-round defence, and in the fifth angle was the blockhouse, originally intended to be enclosed by a bastion projecting into the river. The main firepower was deployed along the river's edge in batteries of guns whose fire crossed with those of the Gravesend Blockhouse. To landward the fort was enclosed by two concentric, water-filled ditches and a covered way; access to the plain, arched landward gate was through two triangular outworks, known as a redan and a ravelin, and then via drawbridges which spanned the ditch in typical Dutch fashion. On the river side was another ornamental gate faced in Portland stone. A similar fort was proposed to enclose the Gravesend Blockhouse, but was never built.

Despite this new work, the absence of forward defences (the blockhouses at Milton, Higham and East Tilbury had been abandoned after 1553) meant that the Thames estuary continued to be vulnerable, and during the third Anglo-Dutch War (1672–4) the Dutch unsuccessfully attempted to close it with blockships.

Artist's impression of Cockham Wood Fort
Victor Smith

The accession, however, of William of Orange to the English throne in 1689 changed the relationship between England and the Netherlands, which became allies. The War of the Grand Alliance (1689–97) ranged them both against the France of Louis XIV. It was in this period that three new batteries, Quaker, Middle and Buda (no traces remain), were built at Grain in the Medway to cross their fire with Sheerness, which was now armed with 150 guns. By the end of the seventeenth century Upnor Castle had become a capacious magazine (in 1691 it was said to contain more gunpowder than any other magazine in England). On the river's edge between it and Cockham Wood, Middleton's and James Batteries (formerly known as Warham and Bay Batteries), were restored, and a new battery was built at Hoo Ness.

Surviving angle of de Gomme's defences at Sheerness
James Chapelard

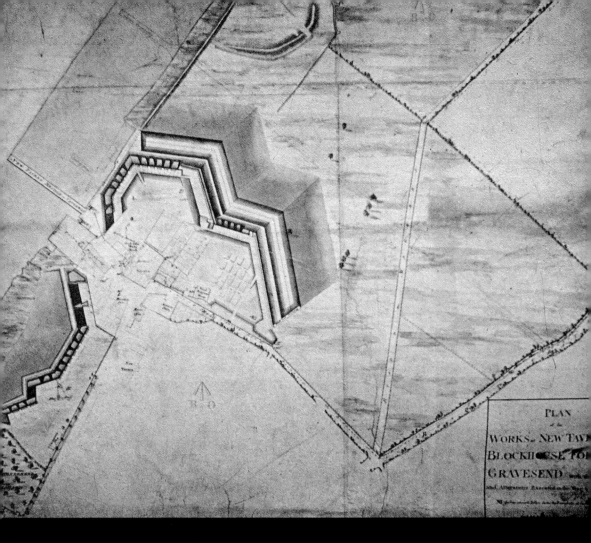

PLAN
of the
WORKS AT NEW TAVE
BLOCKHOUSE FOR
GRAVESEND and Alterations Executed in the Year

The Eighteenth Century

5

Reaction to Continental Wars

Although the English naval victory at La Hogue in 1692 had seemed to lessen the risk of French invasion, the eighteenth century opened with a succession of French invasion scares. Surprisingly, though, Chatham dockyard, which was still expanding, was not fortified until 1755. Then extensive bastioned lines were built on a scale comparable with those existing or under improvement for the dockyards at Portsmouth, Gosport and Plymouth. At this date Dover Castle was also substantially modified for artillery and underwent its most radical alteration in 500 years. This building programme, together with later works, contributed much to the appearance of the castle today. Later in the century, when France allied herself with the insurgent North American colonists during the American War of Independence (1775-1783), the fortification of the Western Heights at Dover was started and a new bastioned line was begun to protect the land front of the dockyard at Sheerness.

The eighteenth century opened with the death of Charles II of Spain, a French claim to the throne of Spain and the resultant War of the Spanish Succession (1701–14) which divided Europe into opposing alliances, with France on one side and most of the rest of Europe (including Britain) on the other. There were French invasion scares in 1707–8, leading to the usual hurried repairs to defences. When the war ended, the arms-

> This building programme, together with later works, contributed much to the appearance of the castle today.

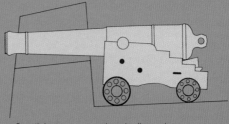

Smooth bore gun on a garrison standing carriage
Victor Smith

reduction clauses of the Treaty of Utrecht (1713) required the number of guns in Kent to be cut by over half, and on the French coast the defences of Dunkirk were also reduced. Standardisation of gun types and mountings in English coastal defences followed. Wherever possible, long-barrelled guns were used (rather than short-barrelled weapons of lesser range), and these were increasingly mounted on standing carriages, like those on ships, instead of the larger field carriages often previously used.

The War of the Austrian Succession (1740–8), in which England and France were again members of opposing alliances, was also attended by French invasion scares. In 1743 an attempted invasion was thwarted by a storm which damaged and sank the transport ships that had been assembled to bring an army across the Channel. The Jacobite Rebellion of 1745 also raised fears of a French intervention, and a plan was drawn up for enclosing London within a continuous rampart with projecting redans, on much the same line as the defences of the English Civil War.

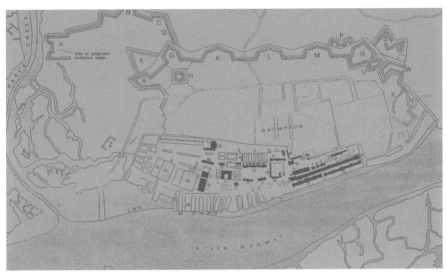

Chatham Lines as altered and extended in the late 18th century
Crown Copyright, NMR

Chatham Lines

The long overdue scheme for defending Chatham dockyard against attack
from the land was begun in 1755, during a period of uneasy peace.
Hitherto, nothing more than a brick wall (of which stretches remain) had
protected the site; this simply prevented illegal access and theft, rather
than provided a defence against attack by troops. The dockyard had
increased in importance, now possessing six building and repair slips, mast
ponds, a rope works and a miscellany of other related structures.

The new defences, designed by the engineer Hugh Debbieg, consisted of
a bastioned line 1½ miles (2.4 km) long on the higher ground above the
dockyard, with return lines to the river bank at either end. Bastioned lines
were a conventional way of defending a dockyard against attack from the
land. The central four of Chatham's eight bastions were of flattish form,
with detached walls behind several sally ports. There were positions for
defensive artillery and a fire-step for musketry defence. The lines were built
of earth and judging from a contemporary plan, had pointed timbers projecting
as an obstruction from their rampart; in front was a defensive ditch.
Construction advanced sufficiently to afford some protection in time for
another French invasion scare in 1756, during the Seven Years War (1756–63).

The lines at Chatham also provided a base from which a field force could
move against an invading army advancing through Kent. Fieldworks, as
used at Chatham, were, however, vulnerable to decay; in 1766 they were
reported to be 'greatly destroyed and rendered almost defenceless by cattle
grazing thereon'. The lines were later made permanent by being reshaped
and clad in brick, and it is in this form that stretches have survived within
the Brompton Barracks and in a military housing estate. They are
considered to be the best surviving bastioned lines of any dockyard in the
United Kingdom.

The eastern defences of Dover Castle
Channel Photography

Dover Castle

Previously there had been only piecemeal additions and adaptations at Dover Castle – one example being the erection of a set of purpose-built barracks around the keep in 1745 (these survive). An extensive programme undertaken in 1755–6 was, however, the first to address the needs of the castle as a whole and its potential for artillery defence.

The defences on the landward approaches from the north and east were improved; the spur outwork north of the castle was remodelled; and between the keep and the Penchester Tower a battery for six guns was built, the medieval towers between Fitzwilliam Gate and Avranches Tower being reduced in height to allow them a reasonable field of fire. A small battery was built just to the north of the church of St Mary in Castro, and numerous other modifications and improvements to ramparts and the ditch defences were made to adapt the castle for modern weapons. A semi-circular battery, just in front of the earlier Mote's Bulwark, also existed by this date. A document of 1756 lists half a dozen more batteries at the castle – from the written context, several of them seem to have faced the harbour and fired on the adjacent beach. The cut-down towers and modified walls remain, but, apart from the one in front of Mote's Bulwark, no trace remains of the seaward-facing batteries.

The end of the Seven Years War in 1763 gave a relatively short-lived respite from fear of invasion. From the later 1770s, though, a succession of wars again raised the spectre of invasion, and, as a result, British defence construction proceeded at an unprecedented pace until the end of the Napoleonic Wars.

Bell Battery and other east facing gun positions at Dover Castle
James Chapelard

Smooth bore guns on Bell Battery
James Chapelard

Mid-18th century barracks in the inner ward of Dover Castle
James Chapelard

Alliances against Britain, which followed the outbreak of the American War of Independence in 1775, placed British military and naval resources under tremendous strain. Britain was on the defensive across the world and trying, with difficulty, to balance the demands of defending its far-flung colonial possessions with the immediate need to protect itself against the threat of French invasion. The state of anxiety which followed the alliance of the French with the insurgent Americans in 1778 led to a combination of urgent holding repairs to existing defences and the building of additional ones.

The year 1779 was one of crisis. The war in the American colonies continued, Gibraltar was under siege by Spain, the American John Paul Jones, following his earlier raiding in 1778, sailed round the British Isles with five ships and captured the British frigate Serapis off the Yorkshire coast, and the French bombarded Elizabeth Castle on Jersey. The presence of a large Franco-Spanish fleet in the English Channel in August 1779 and the reported collection of an army on the coast of France caused great anxiety in Britain. But the enemy fleet withdrew in the face of easterly winds and the danger receded. The émigré French General Dumouriez later told the British that one of the invasion plans had been to land in the Romney Marsh area and then to advance on London. A continuing threat of invasion seemed real enough and in January 1781 a French force landed on Jersey but was repelled.

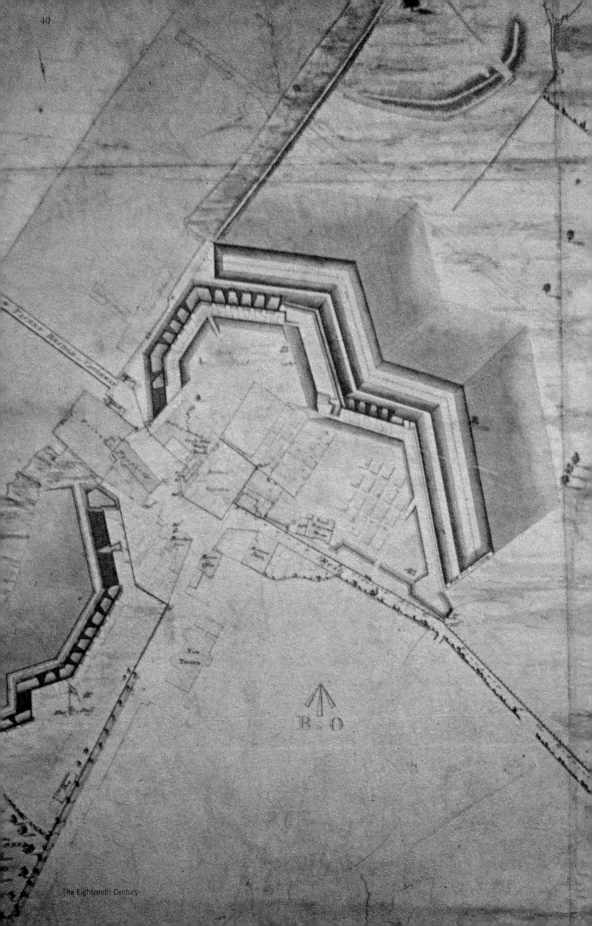

B. O

New defences for Dover and Thanet

Not surprisingly, Dover was in the forefront of defensive preparations. Four seaward-facing batteries were built at harbour level: Guilford Battery, and North, Townshend and Amherst Batteries further west along the waterfront. These were to defend the harbour against attack and the beach against a landing. Nothing of them remains.

The most significant new development at Dover, however, took place across the Dour Valley – on the Western Heights, which were fortified for the first time, to help protect the port against attack and capture from the land. Details are unclear but a plan of 1784 shows that by then the works had progressed to incorporate a self-contained fort at the eastern end of the hill and a citadel to its west, with entrenchments between them. This was the start of a long process which led to the creation of a major fortress on the Western Heights.

In Thanet modest additional batteries were built to defend the small harbours at Broadstairs and Margate. Traces of a battery at Broadstairs survive.

The Thames and Medway

In the Thames the long-overdue upgrading of the defences at Gravesend and Tilbury took place. At Gravesend new earthworks were built: new gun lines, extending east from the Gravesend Blockhouse, and the New Tavern Fort, with its irregular, zigzag plan. The guns of New Tavern faced downstream so as to direct strong long-range fire against enemy warships before they could bring their own guns to bear at shorter range. Nothing is now visible of the Gravesend Blockhouse's gun lines; the plan of New Tavern was perpetuated in later remodelling, although the only feature remaining from its original construction is the brick skin of the medieval Milton Chantry, which became an artillery barracks. On the north side of the river new gun positions were built on the eastern side of Tilbury fort, where emplacements may be traced.

Still no steps were taken to re-establish much-needed forward defences at the eastern end of Gravesend Reach. A proposal made by Captain Hyde Page in 1778 envisaged turning Gravesend into a large entrenched camp, with a citadel on Windmill Hill, to the south of the town. Another plan, made by Colonel Debbieg in 1780, proposed a line of defensive positions to the south of Gravesend and others on rising ground inland of East Tilbury and at Stanford le Hope. Neither proposal was carried out.

The Medway, however, saw significant new work and improvements to existing defences. The new work was at Sheerness, where the expanding dockyard and its associated civil settlement (called 'Blue Town') had outgrown the area enclosed by de Gomme's seventeenth-century defences.

Plan of New Tavern Fort in 1795 (middle), with Gravesend Blockhouse (lower left) and the landward rampart of the Milton Blockhouse (upper right)
Public Record Office

Captain Pitts' design (1783) was for an advanced bastioned line which, like its predecessor, crossed and cut off the dockyard peninsula but was longer and set 750 yards (700 metres) further to landward. It consisted of four earthwork bastions, with connecting curtain walls, fronted by a wide, water-filled ditch, later protected by a ravelin. Although encroached upon by later development, parts of this system may still be seen.

Upstream at Chatham the new square Townshend Redoubt (no longer existing) was built to overlook and strengthen the north end of the existing Lines. A similarly shaped Amherst Redoubt was formed at the southern end, with a hornwork and spur battery being added close by (these were later developed into the Fort Amherst complex of defences). All were predominantly earthworks, and they survive, as later clad in brick, along with much of Chatham Lines. These works powerfully reinforced the land fronts of the two Medway dockyards. As with the Thames defences, there were also contingency plans for field positions – to the south and east of Chatham Lines and north of Upnor Castle and Cockham Wood Fort.

Within ten years of the peace process – involving Britain, the American Congress and its European allies – that ended the American War of Independence with the Peace of Versailles in 1783, the French Revolutionary War broke out, and planning against invasion became more comprehensive and strategic in scope than ever before.

The new advanced bastioned line at Sheerness (lower) and earlier line (upper)
Crown Copyright, NMR

Surviving bastions of the advanced line
Kent County Council

The French Revolutionary and Napoleonic Wars

6

During the French Revolutionary and Napoleonic Wars, Britain faced invasion by forces of unprecedented size, and, for the first time, attempts were made to deny whole lengths of coastline to an enemy. These were vividly expressed in the great Martello tower programme and the cutting of the Royal Military Canal. The defences of Dover Castle and of the Western Heights were also massively strengthened and important new fortifications were built at Chatham and Rochester. All have left substantial remains.

In 1801 troops were assembled at harbours along the French Channel in preparation for a French invasion concentrating on the south-eastern corner of England, especially the favourable landing beaches on the Kent coast.

The French Revolution (1789) produced a political aftershock in England, and further conflict with France was anticipated. A French declaration of war followed in 1793. British fleets were sent to blockade the French ports of Brest, Rochefort and Toulon as well as to cruise the English Channel, as a result of which new defences were built on the French coast in the 1790s, including a line of mainly earthen batteries from Calais to Etaples. The French tried to land forces at Bantry Bay in Ireland in 1796 (the invasion fleet was scattered by a storm), and 1,400 French troops landed at Fishguard in Wales in 1797, but soon surrendered. There was another attempt on Ireland in 1798, when outnumbered French invasion troops were compelled to surrender at Ballinamuck, and the naval squadron carrying a second invasion force was intercepted and defeated in Lough Swilly. These events emphasised the reality of an invasion threat. Indeed in 1801 troops were assembled at harbours along the French Channel in preparation for a French invasion concentrating on the south-eastern corner of England, especially the favourable landing beaches on the Kent coast.

During the Revolutionary and Napoleonic Wars a remarkably extensive new system of defence was built in stages in Kent, involving not just the main centres of the Thames, Medway and Dover but also the building of 35 works to guard 20 miles (32 km) of invasion beaches from Folkestone to Dungeness. But British defence planning became more strategic in scope, too. Civilian resources were brought more into the equation; 'layered' lines of resistance between the coast and London were planned, and so was a 'scorched-earth' policy involving the evacuation of people and livestock from whole areas of the country in the face of an invader. Troop concentrations were established at various points. The new semaphore communication relay system (using movable pointers set on poles erected on high ground within sight of each other) linked London to naval bases and anchorages – including those at Sheerness, Chatham and the Downs – and also, potentially, to military formations in the field. For the first time, this provided the possibility of central control of naval and military forces from a distance. Existing fire beacons to warn of an attack were also retained.

No 2 Battery at Lade
Kent County Council

Coastal defence and traversing gun platforms

Something of a new approach to the defence of coasts was demonstrated at Dungeness, where four widely spaced batteries with the assistance of an inland redoubt, both covered the offshore anchorages and commanded the approaches to its beaches. These batteries, made of shingle contained within brick revetments and internal structures, embodied a distinctive new design that was used for many of the smaller batteries built during the later 1790s in Kent and elsewhere. Their guns were arranged in a faceted arc to seaward, with the rear enclosed by a defensible triangle of walls. The gun carriages were raised on the recently invented timber traversing platforms, an important technological break-through. Moving on a curved metal rail, guns could be rapidly swung on to a target (often through a considerable arc), and – compared with the use of more cumbersome naval-style truck carriages – fewer guns were needed to cover a given area. This became the chief method of mounting guns in forts for almost another century. Of the defences at Dungeness, Battery No. 2 survives at Lade, as does part of No.1 to its south and also much of the redoubt.

This approach was repeated along the coast north to Shorncliffe. Shingle-and-earthwork positions were thrown up immediately north-east of Dungeness, four batteries were built at Hythe, with a fifth at Shorncliffe, and Bayle Battery at Folkestone was revamped (just traceable in later housing); a battery overlooking Folkestone's East Wear Bay has vanished. North of Dover, batteries were added on either side of the forts of the Downs and one survives at Sandwich Bay.

Gun on a typical form of traversing platform
Victor Smith

Traversing gun on the roof of Martello Tower
No 24 at Dymchurch
Victor Smith

Martello towers

Martello Tower No 3 at Folkestone (20th century addition
on its roof)
Chris Parker

During the Napoleonic Wars, which followed the year-long peace of the Treaty of Amiens (1802), defence was dramatically enhanced by the building of a line of Martello gun towers along the coast and by the cutting of the Royal Military Canal. Gun towers had been recommended for the defences of southern England in the later 1790s, and some already existed in the Channel Islands. The Martello towers built along the south-east coast were inspired by a single circular tower at Cape Mortella in Corsica, which in 1794 beat off a determined attack by two British warships and was only captured after troops were landed and field artillery was used to bombard its walls. The sturdy brick towers were built along the coasts from Aldeburgh in Suffolk to Clacton in Essex and in Kent from Folkestone to Romney Marsh, resuming at Rye in Sussex and terminating at Seaford. Others were built in Scotland, Ireland and elsewhere in some of Britain's colonial possessions.

The Essex and Suffolk towers (built 1805–12) were cam-shaped in plan with positions for three traversing guns. Those in Kent (built 1805–8) were elliptical in plan and resembled an upturned flower-pot. Within a circular parapet on the roof was mounted a single heavy gun on a centrally pivoted traversing platform, supported by a substantial round pillar running up from the base of the tower. The basement contained a cistern, at ground level there was a magazine, and on the first floor a barracks. Access to the tower was through a door at first-floor level, reached via a retractable ladder (or, if the tower had an encircling ditch, by a drawbridge).

Most of the south-coast Martello towers were positioned to defend the approaches to invasion beaches and in such cases were built in a line, 500–600 yards (450–550 m) apart, with interlocking fields of fire. This system of defence was made possible by the earlier-mentioned traversing gun platform, which gave the towers a 360° field of fire and allowed speedy rotation for firing to seaward, to the flank, along beaches or inland.

Of the 27 towers built in Kent, 16 survive. The most intact sequence (9) lies on high ground behind the beach from Copt Point, Folkestone, west to Shorncliffe Camp (where the earthwork Shorncliffe Redoubt also survives); the tower at Copt Point is open to visitors. The keep of Sandgate Castle was also adapted as a Martello tower. At Hythe a sequence of 12 towers (the middle 4 remain) ran along the shoreline to the Grand Redoubt at Dymchurch. The latter was built as part of the same programme, and is a low circular brick structure with a central parade ground surrounded by 11 radially placed gun emplacements set over bomb-proof barracks and magazines – the bomb-proofing was for defence against explosive shells fired from bomb ketches. It survives, as modified during World War II, but is in military use, so its interior is inaccessible; a similar redoubt at Eastbourne in Sussex may be visited. The remaining six towers, along the beach to the west of the redoubt, were in three groups guarding the Willop sluice at Dymchurch, the main marshland sluice at the western end of Dymchurch Village and the Globsden Gut sluice. Three survive, including two at Dymchurch Village – one of which is open to visitors.

> Of the 27 towers built in Kent, 16 survive.

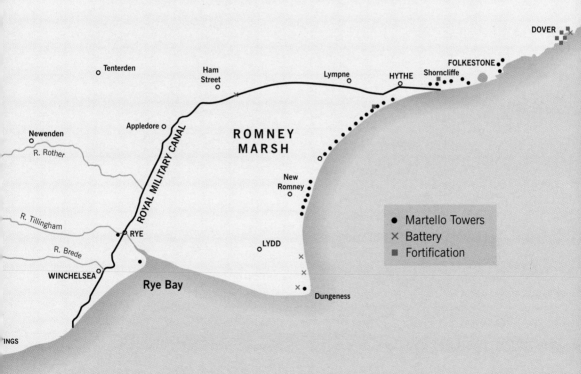

Coastal defences between Dungeness and Dover and the Royal Military Canal

The Royal Military Canal
Kent County Council

The Grand Redoubt at Dymchurch
Kent County Council

■ The French Revolutionary and Napoleonic Wars

The Royal Military Canal

Inland from this line of towers was the Royal Military Canal (cut 1805–7), running along the landward edge of Romney Marsh for 26 miles (42 km) from Hythe to Winchelsea in Sussex. It was a waterway with a towpath on its seaward side and a low rampart backed by a military road to landward. It formed a second line of defence and was cut in a series of stretches, each terminating in a flank which contained a position for a gun that could fire down the next stretch. Aside from its value as an obstacle to invaders, it provided a route for transporting troops and supplies, as did the road that ran behind it. Much of the canal survives, and good stretches may be seen at Hythe and elsewhere, along with the defences which secured its eastern end: the Shorncliffe Battery, a redoubt and a small flanking position.

Dover

Between 1794 and 1805 Dover Castle's eastern defences were massively strengthened by an earthwork formed against the medieval wall, by the widening and deepening of its ditch, and by the construction of four major detached works outside this: Horseshoe, Hudson's, East Demi and East Arrow Bastions. The first three were connected to the castle by tunnels and the last by a tunnel to the castle's east ditch. Within the 'spur' to the north of the castle a triangular outwork was also formed, which was connected to the castle by a bomb-proof gallery (caponier), with gun ports covering the ditch. The 'spur' had a remarkable set of contrivances for controlling the opening and closing of doors to allow the defenders to make a sortie into the ditch. Accommodation, in brick vaults called casemates, was built to the rear of Canon's Gate, and the roof of the Norman keep was also vaulted in brick to support the weight of guns to be placed on its top. All these developments can be seen.

On the Western Heights work continued on defences which were intended not only to protect Dover harbour from attack from the west but also to provide secure accommodation for a field force that could move against any French advance inland from a coastal beachhead. Here the Citadel, North Centre Bastion and Drop Redoubt, with their bombproof barracks, were completed, along with some of the connecting lines. A monumental triple spiral staircase was built to provide rapid three-way transit of troops between the Heights and the harbour area below; this remarkable construction, known as the Grand Shaft, is open to visitors. Despite the money and effort expended on it, though, the system of defensive works on the Western Heights Defences was still incomplete in 1815.

Thanet was considered a possible landing point if the French sought to avoid confrontation with the Dover defences. Ramsgate had two batteries on the cliffs and guns on the pierhead, and near Margate there was Westbrook Battery, apparently on an earlier site. The batteries at Broadstairs continued in use.

The central well of the Grand Shaft, Western Heights at Dover
James Chapelard

The French Revolutionary and Napoleonic Wars

The entrances to the three staircases at the top of the
Grand Shaft
James Chapelard

The Drop Redoubt, Western Heights Defences at Dover
English Heritage

The Thames and Medway

In the later 1790s long-overdue forward batteries were established at the
eastern end of Gravesend Reach (Shornemead, Hope Point and East
Tilbury) on the Thames. These batteries (later demolished) had the
characteristic triangular plan of the period that we have already noted at
Dungeness. At Gravesend a caponier was added at New Tavern Fort for the
defence of its ditch.

In the Medway the new lines at Sheerness were completed, and there was
a massive enlargement of the Chatham Lines. They were extended to St
Mary's Creek and Gillingham Fort (where a brick tower was also added),
increasing their length to nearly 2 miles (3.2 km); this extension was
mutilated in the enlargement of the dockyard in the 1860s and 1870s. The
growing complex at Fort Amherst at the southern end of the lines included
bomb-proof barracks and an underground system with ditch-flanking
casemates. (This site is now a major heritage tourism attraction.)

More radical was the building of new defences - Forts Clarence and Pitt -
to enable the roads and approaches to Rochester Bridge from the south
and east to be cut if needed. Fort Clarence was in effect a road block
extending inland from the riverbank south of Rochester. It took the form
of a 650 yard (600m) long ditch cutting through Borstal Road (over which
there was a drawbridge within a
gatehouse) ending at Maidstone Road
which was controlled by a guardhouse.
A brick tower positioned within the
ditch at a mid point along its length
provided flanking fire in both
directions along the ditch. The tower,
whose roof protruded above the
counterscarp, contained a small
casemated barrack. Where the ditch
began at the Medway was another,
smaller tower. Sections of the ditch
and its central tower remain.

The French Revolutionary and Napoleonic War

The Fort Amherst complex at the southern end of Chatham Lines
Kent County Council

To the east was built Fort Pitt, a large detached work on a hill overlooking the dockyard, and a pair of small outlying works known as Delce and Gibraltar Towers; these controlled other road access to Rochester bridge and denied an enemy the commanding high ground above the dockyard. Fort Pitt was a four-bastioned work, fronted by a triangular outwork or ravelin on its south side and by a casemated barracks on the north, with a two-storey gun tower at its centre. Parts of the fort, including two bastions joined by a curtain wall, survive in the grounds of a school, and some brick traces of Delce Tower also survive. Like Dover, Chatham had become a base from which an army could attack an invader marching on the capital through Kent.

Planning of successive lines of resistance between the coast and London continued. An inner line was to enclose the capital, and there is a suggestion that fieldworks were established on Shooters Hill at Woolwich and on Blackheath.

After Waterloo

7

Forts and Technology

In the decades after 1815 the small amount of new defence building in Kent included the earliest known fully-developed example in Britain of a fort built in the new polygonal style. At the entrance to the Medway a late version of a Martello tower was erected offshore. By the later 1850s, though, advances in military and naval technology had rendered many of Britain's existing defences obsolete. This situation coincided with a revived fear of invasion from France, now under Napoleon III. As a result, the report of the Royal Commission on the Defence of the United Kingdom (1860) led to the inception of the most extensive and expensive

Elevation and half-section of Fort Darnet in the Medway
David Barnes

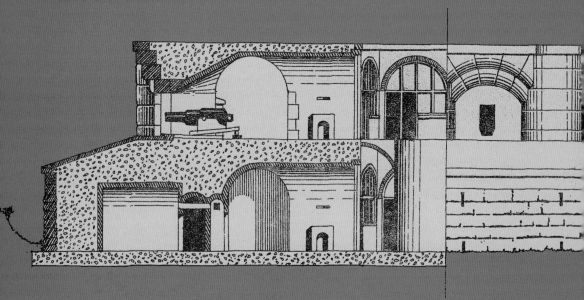

programme of defence construction yet undertaken in Britain, of which key elements were in Kent.

In the years of peace after the Napoleonic Wars, work on the construction of forts and batteries was either rapidly completed or suspended. In something of an anti-climax, the defences were placed on a 'care-and-maintenance' basis and mostly disarmed. Along the coasts some of the Martello towers were turned over to the'Coast Blockade' (later the Coastguard), to help combat smuggling. Others were locked up. The guns of the Royal Military Canal were preserved in sheds, and the canal was used for commercial transport to help offset the costs of maintenance. Squatters occupied some forts and batteries.

Despite its defeat, France showed remarkable powers of recovery, and there were further invasion scares in 1825 and in 1830. These stimulated a burst of further defence planning but no new construction. In the ensuing decades, the French built new fortifications along their Channel coast, some of which may be seen at Boulogne and Calais. Around Dunkirk a new bastioned wall was built in 1818 to protect the harbour and town.

Later on, the effects of the Industrial Revolution worked their way through to the application of steam power to warships. Such ships would be less dependent than their predecessors on wind and tide, so the threat of troop-laden French steamers appearing at any time, and without warning, began to cause concern. As part of an enhancement of the naval defences, Dover was earmarked in 1840 as a harbour of refuge for the fleet, and in 1847 work began on the building of the Admiralty Pier.

In the years of peace after the Napoleonic Wars, work on the construction of forts and batteries was either rapidly completed or suspended.

Polygonal fortification comes to Kent

An invasion panic in 1847–8, a revolution in France in 1848 and Napoleon III's coup in the same year produced a political crisis that prompted new defence construction in the Thames and at Dover.

Shornemead Fort, on the south bank of the Thames, built in the middle of this crisis (1848–52), introduced to Kent the new polygonal style of fortification. This rejected angular bastioned forms and its complicated geometry, substituting a simpler straight-lined plan for the ramparts. Bomb-proof vaults called caponiers, lower in height than the ramparts and pierced with firing positions, projected into the ditch for close-range defence. Caponiers had already appeared as features added to the defences of Dover Castle and at New Tavern Fort, Gravesend. This new defensive form achieved an easier and more efficient division of fire by freeing all the rampart space for long-range firing. Theoretical inspiration for this approach derived from a questioning of past practice in the treatises of several French engineers (including Montalembert in the later eighteenth century) who sought in various ways to find answers to the problems of the bastioned system. Nonetheless, France persisted with bastioned fortification until later in the nineteenth century, although the Prussians adopted the new system enthusiastically from early in the century, applying it in the rings of detached forts that they began to construct around towns and other strategic points.

The British feared the obsolescence of their existing 'wooden wall' warships and their forts.

The fort at Shornemead was a single, isolated example of the new design used for river defence – though it might well have been acceptable as one of a line of forts on a land front. It was pentagonal in plan (a common shape for polygonal forts), the three faces against the river armed with heavy guns and the two to landward forming a defensible barracks. Caponiers with loopholes projected into the ditch, and further flanking fire into the rear ditch could be directed from the barracks. Sadly, this milestone in British military architecture no longer exists. Just ten years after its completion it was demolished to make way for a replacement fort in the 1860s.

In the Medway, at Grain Spit, a late version of a Martello tower was built in 1855. This powerful structure, in granite-faced brick, was armed with three guns on traversing platforms mounted on its roof. Its elliptical plan resembles the earlier towers of Kent and Sussex, but the trio of guns on its roof is reminiscent of the Suffolk and Essex towers. With later additions, it remains a prominent feature of the entrance to the Medway.

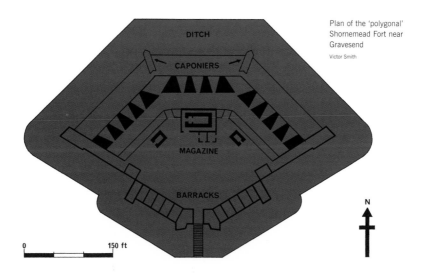

DITCH

CAPONIERS

MAGAZINE

BARRACKS

0   150 ft

Plan of the 'polygonal' Shornemead Fort near Gravesend

Victor Smith

N

Caponier of the Drop Redoubt Western Heights defences at Dover
James Chapelard

The fixing of a casemate shield during the 1860s
Royal Engineers Library

Technological and political imperatives

Yet, even as the Grain Spit Tower was being built, new technological threats were emerging – ironclad warships and rifled-bore artillery – and, in reaction to them, a massive new national programme of coastal defence soon followed. The problem for British defence planners was how to deal with the threat to existing coastal defences that would be posed by the new and more powerful rifled guns in which a spiral groove in the bore of the gun imparted a rotary motion to a new type of pointed cylindrical projectile. Using improved gunpowder charges, these guns could fire considerably further, more accurately and more destructively than smooth-bore weapons. If foreign navies mounted such guns on the new steam ironclads – which were impervious to the roundshot fired from the smooth-bore guns equipping most British defences at the time -– the threat would be all the greater.

Portents of the future had been shown during the Crimean War (1854–6), with the use of armoured floating batteries by the French and the employment of rifled guns. The British feared the obsolescence of their existing 'wooden wall' warships and their forts. When France began a programme of manufacturing rifled artillery, and in 1858 launched the ironclad Gloire, this technological threat took on an even greater sense of immediacy. Moreover, the French construction of the Suez Canal, together with the enhancement of her naval and military capacity, was seen as implying a geopolitical agenda of aggrandisement and an intention to challenge Britain. Furthermore, a massive new harbour was built for the naval base at Cherbourg with forts on the moles (which can still be seen), and after the Franco-German War of 1870 the artillery defences of Boulogne, Calais and Dunkirk were modernised. Britain, though, had the money and the industrial capacity to outbuild the French. This led Parliament to undertake a massive and unprecedented programme to modernise the fleet, symbolised by the launching of the ironclad HMS Warrior in 1860, and to build or rebuild many of the nation's coastal defences and arm them with the new rifled guns. The fortification element of this programme was planned by a Royal Commission set up in 1859 to consider the requirements for the defence of the United Kingdom.

Grain Fort (lower) and the later Wing Battery (upper)
Kent County Council

Hoo Fort
Kent County Council

Its members were mainly military officers but included a naval officer to represent naval interests and a senior civil servant from the Treasury. Its report in 1860 recommended a massive new scheme of fortification for Portsmouth, Spithead, Plymouth, Pembroke, Dover, Chatham and the Medway, Woolwich and the Thames, as well as for Cork in Ireland. Although the Royal Commission scheme was twice reduced in extent by Parliament on cost grounds, no fewer than 76 new forts were built or rebuilt, involving many sites in Kent.

Slough Fort, Allhallows
Kent County Council

Replica rifled muzzle-loader at New Tavern Fort, Gravesend
Victor Smith

The Royal Commission forts

In the 1860s, as part of the Royal Commission scheme, three new forts were built at the eastern end of Gravesend Reach to form the advance defences of the River Thames, starkly imposing their vertical masonry forms upon the marshscape. Shornemead, built on the site of the 1852 fort, and Cliffe on the south bank, and Coalhouse at East Tilbury on the north bank demonstrated Britain's response to the changing technological circumstances. They were 'state of the art' defences for their day, incorporating the latest technology: the rifled guns were mounted inside casemates having massive frontal protection of granite and iron plate, and overhead cover of thick concrete to withstand bombardment fire, although unprotected open embrasures were permitted at the less vulnerable up-river end. The American Civil War of 1861–5, in which rifled guns reduced ordinary brick-and-masonry forts to rubble, seemed to confirm the need for this approach. Advances in mechanical engineering were incorporated in the form of all-metal traversing platforms for the guns and hand-geared machinery for elevating and turning them on to their targets. Mid-nineteenth-century heavy engineering and foundry improvements meant that the guns – powerful bottle-shaped muzzle-loaders – were also of unprecedented size and weight, ranging from 9" to $12\frac{1}{2}$" (23 cm to 32 cm) in calibre, and weighing from 12 to 38 tons. They could fire projectiles weighing between 200 lb (90 kg) and nearly half a ton over ranges of up to 3 miles (4.9 km). These shells were brought up by mechanical ammunition

Because of the increasing range of artillery, the land fronts of fortresses had to be built further out, so as to increase the protection they could give against land-based attack.

The defences at Garrison Point, Sheerness
Kent County Council

lifts from well-protected magazines, sited deep beneath the casemates, which incorporated safety lighting (candle lanterns behind plate glass). A defensible barracks constructed of Kentish rag blockwork closed the rear of the forts, and their front ditches were defended by caponiers.

These massive structures were forts of an industrial age, and their guns could compete on equal terms with any warship then in service. Cliffe and Coalhouse Forts remain entire, but only the façade of the casemated front of Shornemead exists (although its partially demolished condition is very instructive in revealing the layered nature of its construction). New Tavern and Tilbury Forts were also remodelled. Some of their emplacements were also protected by iron shields (one emplacement at New Tavern Fort has recently been rearmed with a replica gun). Well downstream at Allhallows a miniature version of a casemated fort (Slough Fort, which still survives) was built to provide a link between the Thames and Medway defences and to prevent a landing on the sands in front of it.

In the Medway, similar designs were adopted for the construction of the massive and monumental fort at Garrison Point (one of only two double-tiered armoured and casemated forts built in Britain) and for two circular forts upstream on Hoo and Darnet islands. Rebuilt open emplacements along the old seaward-facing lines of Sheerness had a lesser standard of protection. Across the river at Grain two works (Grain Fort and Grain Battery, connected by a sunken covered way) crossed their fire with Sheerness. All these forts are traceable in varying degrees of preservation.

Because of the increasing range of artillery, the land fronts of fortresses had to be built further out, so as to increase the protection they could give against land-based attack. This made continuous defence lines – like those adopted earlier at Chatham and Sheerness – too expensive, and rings of detached, mutually supporting polygonal forts with interlocking fields of fire were preferred. Ring fortresses were built in the 1860s to defend the landward approaches to the great dockyards at Portsmouth and Plymouth,

Cliffe Fort
Kent County Council

and in Kent the Royal Commission proposed a ring fortress for the land defence of Chatham, together with a connecting line of forts from the western bank of the Medway, passing north via Gad's Hill to the Thames at Shornemead. This was, however, delayed on cost grounds (the idea of the line of the Thames being abandoned), which also caused the dropping of a scheme for land defences at Woolwich. However, at about this date or a little earlier a small battery was built on the riverbank at Woolwich dockyard; this remains, armed with traversing guns.

Detached forts were also proposed to cover the land approaches to Sheerness, but instead an outdated linear defence was provided in the form of the Queenborough Lines, which ran for 2 miles (3.2 km) coast to coast from West Minster to Barton's Point. The Lines took the form of a low earthen rampart fronted by a wide, wet ditch, defended along its length from two short flanks near the centre and by works at its ends. (The Hilsea Lines, between Portsmouth dockyard and the new outer ring of forts at Portsdown, are another example of a linear defence built during this period.)

The two-tiered casemates of Garrison Point Fort, Sheerness
James Chapelard

The interior of the casemates at Cliffe Fort
Kent County Council

Queenborough Lines, Sheppey
Kent County Council

Dover

Improvements at Dover enhanced its importance and strengthened its role as a strategic fortress, whose garrison could act against an invader marching through Kent. The Western Heights defences were finally completed, the castle was upgraded, and a large polygonal work, Fort Burgoyne, was built to the north of it.

Fort Burgoyne defended the northern approaches to the castle and, at long range, covered the north front of the Western Heights. Its plan was that of a flattened chevron, with several raised gun casemates on the ramparts, and behind it, a large V-shaped earthwork facing south towards the castle; an unusual feature was the wing ramparts extending from either flank and leading to two outlying redoubts. The ditch of the fort was defended by caponiers, and its revetments display early use of concrete, a material that would have an increasingly important role to play in the construction of defensive works. Fort Burgoyne is at present in military occupation.

At the west end of the Western heights a massive new work with caponiers, called the Western Outwork, was added. At the same time, caponiers were added to the Drop Redoubt at the east end of the Heights, and the main line of ditches was extended east from it to the edge of the cliffs. With other caponiers and gun positions in revetments to flank the ditches, the Western Heights had evolved into a large and impressive fortress with a system of ramparts and ditches 3 miles (4.9 km) long. A public footpath provides some access to this nationally important heritage site.

Dover Castle's seaward defences, for protecting the harbour, were also upgraded with positions for 15 heavy, rifled muzzle-loaders (East Demi Bastion, Hospital, Shot Yard and Shoulder of Mutton Batteries). Their height above the sea meant that they were less vulnerable to direct fire, so protection by iron armour was not considered necessary. Archcliffe Fort received similar weapons, most of them conventionally mounted on traversing platforms, but with one on an ingenious counterweighted carriage which rose up to fire and on recoil disappeared below the parapet for reloading. This reflected the latest inventiveness in heavy engineering as applied to gunnery. Close by was South Lines Battery, which mounted guns on traversing platforms.The elevated St Martin's Battery on the Western Heights was similarly provided.

Elsewhere in Kent, only remnants of the batteries built along the coastline in the Revolutionary and Napoleonic Wars remained in use. Battery No. 1 at Dungeness was rearmed with rifled guns, and several Martello towers and the Dymchurch Grand Redoubt still mounted guns, as did Sandgate Castle and Folkestone Battery. Although little maintained, the Royal Military Canal continued to be perceived as a defensive obstacle

The Chatham Ring Fortress

8

A Continental comparison: M. Mougin's design for an underground French fort with guns in cupolas

By 1875 money had finally been found to build the land fortress to
defend Chatham dockyard. In the course of its construction a new
doctrine for British land fortresses evolved, based on decentralised
defensive methods and moveable armaments.

As originally planned, this ring of detached and mutually supporting
forts was to have been formed of seven polygonal works of the same type
as those built at Portsmouth and Plymouth in the 1860s. The forts were
to occupy the best terrain for commanding the land approaches to
Chatham dockyard in an arc from the Medway Valley at Borstal to the
riverbank at Twydall. They were positioned $1^{1}/_{2}$ miles (2.5 km) from the
dockyard. This distance, set in 1860, reflected the increased range
expected of enemy guns and the need to keep those guns at a distance –
though further increases in the range of artillery had made even this
distance too little by the time building of the forts began.

Construction commenced in 1875, with a start on the first four of the
forts south of the Chatham Valley (Borstal, Bridgewoods, Horsted and
Luton). But for a stop in the work at the end of the 1870s because of a
shortage of funds, these might well have been completed, incorporating
now out-of-date features, such as caponiers and exposed faces, that can
be seen in the forts of the Portsmouth and Plymouth rings. When work
resumed in the 1880s, however, the continuing development and
increasing power of both artillery and small arms had caused the
assumptions that had guided the designers of the late 1860s and early
1870s, to be questioned, modified and eventually overturned. A new
land fortress system had evolved.

The largest of the forts was Horsted. It had a regular chevron plan and
was surrounded by a deep ditch. There were, however, no caponiers for
ditch defence, as such exposed cross-ditch structures had become more
vulnerable to accurate, high-angle, indirect fire from the new howitzers
and mortars being introduced into continental service. Instead, positions

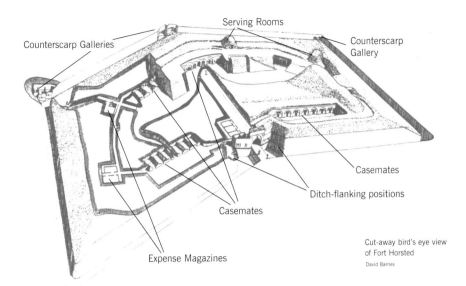

Counterscarp Galleries

Serving Rooms

Counterscarp Gallery

Casemates

Ditch-flanking positions

Casemates

Expense Magazines

Cut-away bird's eye view
of Fort Horsted
David Barnes

for defending the ditch were made less vulnerable by recessing them into their revetments. Another new feature was the use of concrete for structures under mounded chalk rubble and earth. Accommodation and stores were protected in casemates under the front and rear ramparts, and a mounded-over tunnel bisecting the fort served as a gun store and contained the main magazines, as well as acting as a traverse. The slightly smaller Forts Borstal and Bridgewoods and the much smaller Fort Luton were asymmetrical in shape but followed the same general approach. At Borstal a caponier was added in the less vulnerable rear ditch, but Luton had no provision for ditch defence.

Changes such as these represented only a stage in the evolution of existing thinking on fixed defences

Changes such as these represented only a stage in the evolution of existing thinking on fixed defences. The increasing power of artillery, along with lessons from recent experience of warfare also led to new thinking in the approach to the positioning and use of defensive artillery. The invulnerability of fixed armaments began to be questioned. At Plevna in 1878 the Turks had used extemporised dugouts and fieldworks defended

The defensible entrance of Fort Bridgewoods (demolished)
Victor Smith

by repeating rifles to resist Russian assaults, and this example was influential in moving the minds of planners in England away from the idea of basing the defence of a land front upon permanent forts. The original intention for the Chatham forts had been to mount heavy fixed guns on the ramparts, served by lifts

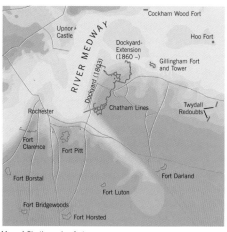

Map of Chatham ring fortress
After David Barnes

from the underlying magazines, but an alternative method of defence was now adopted, based on less vulnerable dispersed artillery. When work was resumed in 1886-9 to complete Chatham's ring of defences, some of the new thinking was implemented at Twydall, to the east of Gillingham, where, instead of artillery forts, two infantry redoubts were built; the artillery was to be dispersed to concealed positions nearby. The redoubts were of low profile, with buried bomb-proof shelters and a concealed ditch set with an 'unclimbable' fence. This distinctive form, practically invisible to an enemy until he was at close range, became known as the Twydall profile and was used elsewhere in British coastal defences and even by the Russians in China.

The defensive scheme for the whole of the Chatham fortress was then revised to provide for heavy guns to be dispersed, and for the forts to be equipped with light, mobile armaments that could be moved to concealed positions outside, once an enemy had established his breaching batteries. Fort Darland (1899), the last of the Chatham ring, was an infantry work for machine-guns but with a moveable armament. It also had a rear caponier to carry an entrance bridge.

The Chatham fortress had evolved into a defensive system in which the use of artillery and rapid-fire rifles and machine-guns in dispersed and concealed positions was given a real and decisive place. Even the land fronts of Dover, Portsmouth and Plymouth began to be adapted to the new thinking with the use of moveable guns. This contrasted with continental practice on frontiers and other land fronts, which initially responded to the new circumstances by retaining fixed guns in forts but giving them increased and expensive protection in either steel cupolas or armoured casemates (as at Namur and Liège in Belgium, Verdun in France and at Bucharest in Romania). However, some continental practice also moved to decentralised forms of defence, pioneered by Germany's Feste groups of batteries.

Of the Chatham ring, Borstal, Horsted and Luton survive intact, with fragmentary traces of Darland in a housing estate and of the redoubts at Twydall in farmland.

The Twydall Profile
Victor Smith

■ The Chatham Ring Fortress

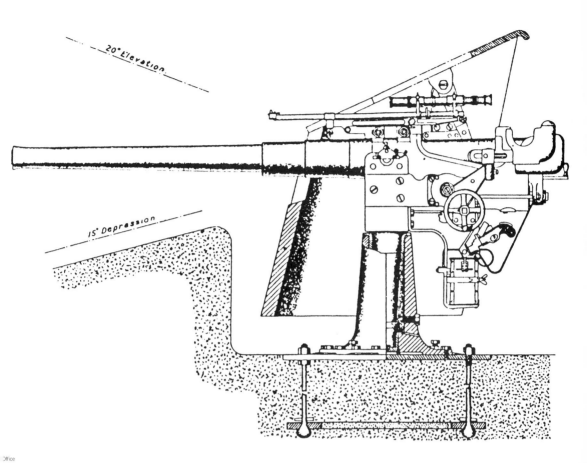

20° Elevation

15° Depression

Office

Technology Marches on

9

Breech-loaders for Coastal Defence

Building on earlier improvements, advances in military technology
accelerated during the later nineteenth century, resulting in the introduction
of effective breech-loading guns, electric searchlights, telephone and
telegraphic communications and in new fire-control techniques. These and
other developments revolutionised coastal defence methods and led to the
complete replacement of guns and gun-control systems. Evidence of this may
be seen on the Thames and the Medway and at Dover.

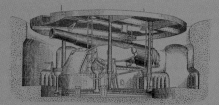

Disappearing gun in retracted and firing positions

The Dover turret

Shortly before this technological transition, a curiosity appeared at Dover.
This was the iron-plated Dover turret, a circular rotating structure weighing
over 700 tons built in 1878 on the Admiralty Pier but not armed until 1882
or handed over to the Royal Artillery until 1886. It mounted two 16-inch
(40-cm) rifled muzzle-loaders, weighing 80 tons, which could fire over ranges
of up to 4 miles (7 km). Steam engines powered traversing, elevating and
loading. The muzzle-loaders, however, were already outdated when installed,
but, nonetheless, the turret and its guns survive: a remarkable tribute to
Victorian engineering.

  The use of turrets at sea during the American Civil War had aroused
interest, and a sprinkling of them for British defences had been envisaged in
1860 – it was even suggested that one should be erected on the keep of Dover
Castle. Although turrets were used in the land defences of some other states,
the Dover example did not presage their adoption for British coastal defences.

An earlier form of disappearing carriage for a rifled
muzzle-loader

The raising of a giant gun for mounting in the Dover Turret
Crown Copyright/MOD

A 6-in breech-loader mounted at New Tavern Fort, Gravesend, in one of the new types of concrete emplacement
Victor Smith

From the end of the 1890s Germany too began to be seen as a significant menace

New systems of defence

From the 1880s advances in science and its application to military technology, combined with Franco-British competition for the acquisition of colonies and the risk of war between the two powers, helped instigate an 'arms race'. From the end of the 1890s Germany too began to be seen as a significant menace. With a plethora of 'invasion' fiction and scare-mongering literature also fomenting an atmosphere of threat and public anxiety, the French and German military and naval programmes were perceived as a challenge to Britain, and this led to a determined effort to expand the fleet and modernise the seaward defences of dockyards and key harbours.

The invention of the interrupted-screw thread for breech mechanisms led to the gradual introduction of effective breech-loading guns that, compared with muzzle-loaders, fired at a rate of rounds per minute – instead of minutes per round – and had a much greater range of up to 7 miles (11km), or more. Warships had now evolved from steam and sail vessels, mounting muzzle-loaders, to significantly more powerful, fully-fledged armoured steamers provided with breech-loaders. Together with the development of the more destructive high-explosive fillings for projectiles (and subsequently the use of smokeless propellants), breech-loaders thus revolutionised artillery on land and sea. In addition, the use of optics and electro-mechanical engineering was now combined with trigonometry to allow accurate targeting and range-finding for guns (which resulted in the establishment of fire-control positions in batteries), and the combination of electricity-generation with the new carbon-arc technology led to the use of searchlights, which allowed guns to fire at targets at night. Searchlight emplacements are visible at a number of sites. Telephones and the electric telegraph also allowed for more rapid and effective communication and for the tactical control of groups of guns from remotely-placed observation cells.

Muzzle-loaders were retained for a time, but in Britain's ten-year programme of modernisation, from the middle of the 1890s, most new development took the form of batteries for breech-loaders. Like the earlier Royal Commission forts in Kent, these were concentrated on the Thames, the Medway and Dover. Because of the increasing range of guns, there was an emphasis, in the Thames and Medway, on siting guns further downstream, relegating upstream batteries to second-line status. At Dover, batteries were thrown out on the flanks to extend artillery coverage.

Range Finder

Range finding by triangulation
Victor Smith

The process began with the mounting of light quick-firers and electric searchlights at existing batteries– to guard against the new fast torpedo boats whose predatory incursions were especially feared – before more substantive development ensued. As with the land fronts of fortresses, the design of the new batteries rejected the monumentalism of the 1860s in favour of less visible forms. Fed from underlying magazines provided with the latest mechanical ammunition lifts, guns on centrally pivoted mountings, in concrete pits, fired over a parapet through a wide arc of fire – which allowed a greater area of water to be covered with fewer weapons. This approach was applied both to new sites and to the modernisation of earlier works (where old and visible vertical fronts were sometimes disguised by embanking them). It was also adopted in French and other continental defences, for example at Dunkirk, Calais, Boulogne and Cherbourg.

Coast defence searchlight emplacement at Garrison Point, Sheerness
James Chapelard

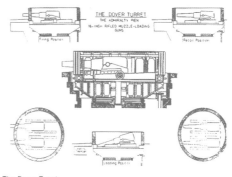

The Dover Turret
John Guy

The Thames and Medway

On the Essex shore of the Thames one of a new genre of concealed batteries incorporating the Twydall profile was built in 1891–2 at East Tilbury. Its six heavy long-range guns, like those in the batteries added either side of Slough Fort (1895) at Allhallows on the Kent side, were on disappearing carriages. These feats of engineering – a more advanced form of the disappearing carriage previously mounted at Dover – used hydro-pneumatics to power a cycle of firing, recoil into concealment within a pit, and raising again for firing. Few of these expensive systems were built. Most development took the form of less complicated, cheaper low-profile barbette mountings, like those provided at Tilbury, Coalhouse, Cliffe and New Tavern Forts, where emplacements survive (at New Tavern Fort the two-gun battery has been restored and rearmed). To defend the river minefields and boom defences that would be established in time of war, smaller batteries with electric searchlights were added south of Coalhouse Fort in Essex and on the Kentish shore at Lower Hope

Similar processes applied in the Medway, where heavy guns were mounted at Sheerness, at Ravelin Battery (demolished) and Barton's Point (partly extant). Guns were also added to the roof of the Garrison Point Fort and to seaward-facing lines. Across the river at Grain, breech-loaders were emplaced on the ramparts of the existing Grain Fort and Grain Battery, and two new batteries were added nearby. Upstream, the channel north of Burntwick Island was defended by a boom, at either end of which emplacements for light quick-firers and searchlights were built (North and South Boom batteries; the latter survives).

Long breakwaters were built from 1904 to extend the naval harbour of refuge

Gun emplacement on the detached breakwater at Dover
Victor Smith

The eastern entrance of Dover Harbour
Victor Smith

Dover and its new harbour

At Dover two long-range batteries were built for heavy guns: Citadel Battery, which survives just beyond the end of the Western Outwork on the Western Heights, and Langdon Battery, east of the Castle, which remains as altered for its conversion into the Dover Strait coastguard station. South Front Battery was built on the western side of Dover – it was succeeded in 1909 by new guns emplaced next to the defunct Dover turret – and other new gun positions were added at the Castle. Long breakwaters were built from 1904 to extend the naval harbour of refuge: two arms projecting from the land and a central detached breakwater. The entrances were equipped for a boom defence, and at the ends of the breakwaters were guns mounted in concrete emplacements, with searchlights, quarters and magazines (much of which survives).

Submarine mining and the Brennan torpedo

Mining defence was based on the use of floating or submerged explosive-filled containers that either exploded on contact with the hull of an enemy vessel or were detonated electrically from look-out posts on the shore. Minefields were especially effective for defending rivers and harbours, and were often linked with boom defences. They were usually protected by quick-firing guns, aided by searchlights, to prevent enemy attempts to clear the mines. The Thames, Medway and Dover were all provided with mines in peacetime, ready to be deployed in war.

A short-lived measure was the Brennan torpedo, introduced in the 1890s. This was a powered vehicle with a guncotton warhead; it was aimed from the land, on which was a steam winch that unwound two drums of wire in its hull, linked to propellers which drove the weapon through the water to explode against its target. The wires were for both steering and propulsion. The remains of control positions and launching ramps may be seen at Cliffe Fort on the Thames and Garrison Point Fort on the Medway, the only two Brennan torpedo stations established in Kent.

By around 1905 Kent's coastal defences had been transformed from obsolescence into a powerful, modern system that formed the basis of the coastal defences in the county for the next fifty years.

Eastern torpedo launching bay, Cliffe Fort
Victor Smith

A short-lived measure was the Brennan torpedo, introduced in the 1890s.

Brennan Torpedo
Royal Engineers Museum

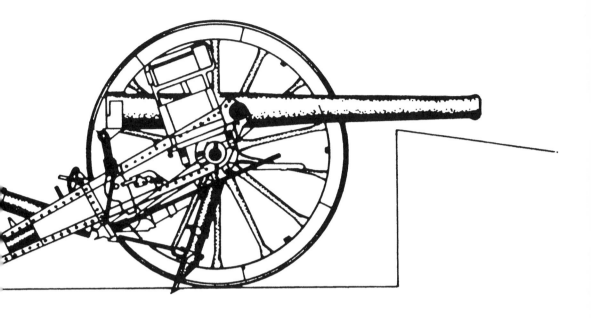

London's Land Defences

Paper and concrete

10

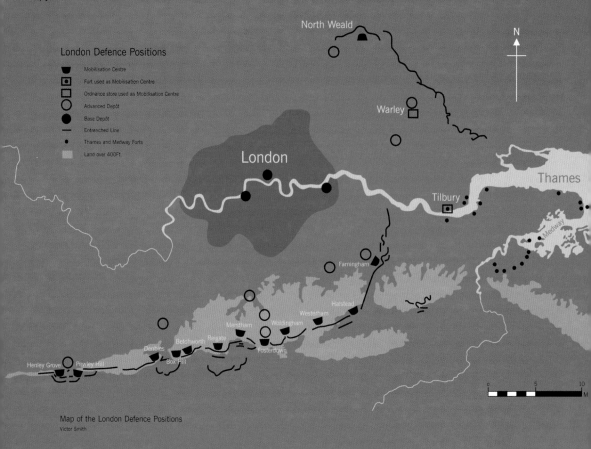

London Defence Positions

- ▼ Mobilisation Centre
- ▣ Fort used as Mobilisation Centre
- ▢ Ordnance store used as Mobilisation Centre
- ○ Advanced Depôt
- ● Base Depôt
- — Entrenched Line
- • Thames and Medway Forts
- ▨ Land over 400Ft.

North Weald

Warley

London

Thames

Tilbury

Medway

Farningham

Halstead

Westerham

Merstham   Woldingham

Denbies   Betchworth   Reigate

Henley Grove   Pewley Hill   Box Hill   Fosterdown

N

0   5   10
M

Map of the London Defence Positions
Victor Smith

Fear of French invasion in the 1880s led to the adoption of a contingency plan for large-scale land defences for London. This involved the building of some permanent works.

London was the prime target for capture by an invader, but, since the decay of the Civil War fieldworks of the 1640s, successive proposals to protect it with permanent fortifications had been rejected because of their excessive cost. By the later 1880s, however, when a revived threat of invasion from France was perceived, an affordable alternative method of defence had emerged. This was in effect a large-scale contingency plan for defence that combined limited permanent construction 'before the event' with paper planning for work to be carried out only when the threat materialised.

The earmarking of prepared positions not to be occupied or utilised until a period of emergency was also a feature of some of the expensively constructed permanent ring fortresses on the continent. The difference with the London plan was that this was nearly its whole basis. The strategy was not to confront an invader on the beaches but to attack as he advanced inland – for which purpose five army corps and twelve cavalry brigades were allocated, with ten infantry and three cavalry divisions held in reserve within the London defences.

Paper and concrete

The paper plan envisaged an entrenched line 116 km (72 miles) long, located well out from the capital, to be established by contract labour only in the event of an actual invasion emergency (optimistically,

15-pounder breech-loading field gun as allocated to the London Defences
Victor Smith

just four days were allowed for this). It would run along the escarpment of the North Downs from Guildford to Westerham, then up the Darenth Valley to the Thames, resuming at Vange in Essex and continuing to Epping; there were to be outlying positions in front of the gaps in the Downs at Guildford, Box Hill and Redhill, with a further position on Wrotham Hill in Kent. This line was to be armed with 400 mobile guns. The permanent construction took the form of a sequence of 13 structures that were built along the intended line in the 1890s. These combined the roles of prepared defensive positions and of magazines containing ammunition for the artillery that would be deployed along the escarpment in an invasion emergency, plus a reserve of entrenching and other tools. They were the prepared focal points for the entrenchments of the defence line, which were to be thrown up between them – although they were referred to as 'mobilisation centres' in contemporary Parliamentary statements (probably out of political expediency, to avoid admitting that, in effect, fortifications were being built).

  The three permanent works in Kent – at Farningham, Halstead and Westerham – were infantry redoubts (it was intended to add quick-firing artillery at Halstead). Farningham, which had a somewhat bunker-like appearance, repeated the Twydall profile; it was a semi-circular work with a

Fear of French invasion in the 1880s led to the adoption of a contingency plan for large-scale land defences for London.

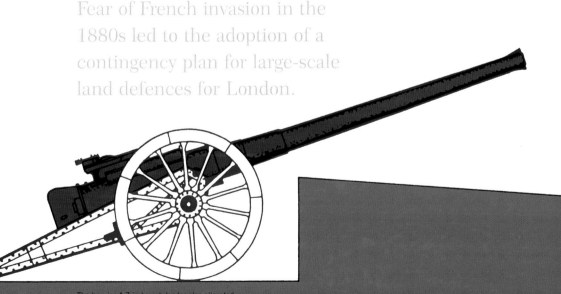

The heavier 4.7-in breech-loader also allocated
Victor Smith

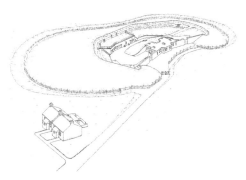

Westerham Mobilisation Centre
Roger Gill, Palmerston Forts Society

rifle parapet on an earthen rampart sloping to a shallow V-shaped ditch containing a steel fence. Under the rampart were storage magazines; and casemates and a loopholed flank wall linking the ends of the ramparts closed the rear of the position; behind it were a detached mobilisation tool store and a caretaker's cottage. The most expensive of all the London defences was Halstead. An eleven-sided structure with a central traverse, it had a concrete revetted ditch and a properly formed rampart with underlying casemates and magazines. Spaces on the rampart seem to have been provided for moveable armament. Westerham was closer in design to Farningham. Halstead survives on secure government property. Westerham has been mutilated but Farningham is in better condition, even though its ditch has been infilled. Both are private property.

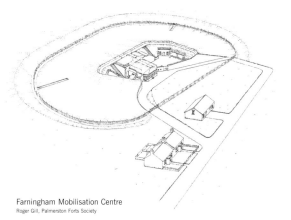

Farningham Mobilisation Centre
Roger Gill, Palmerston Forts Society

   The value of extemporised defences such as this plan envisaged was driven home during the Boer War by the devastating effects of small-arms fire directed from entrenchments, and also by the Russian defence of Port Arthur against the Japanese in 1905. It was to be confirmed during World War I on the Western Front, where the fighting was, in effect, protracted fortress warfare on an unprecedented scale.

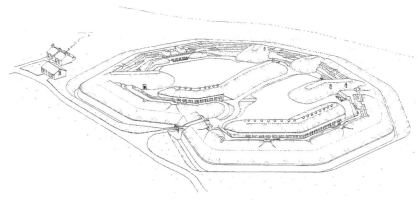

Fort Halstead near Sevenoaks
Roger Gill, Palmerston Forts Society

World War I

Defence against attack from the sea
Land fronts
Defence against air attack

11

Defensive trench on Sheppey
Royal Engineers Museum

Field emplacement on Sheppey
Royal Engineers Museum

The coastal batteries built between 1895–1905 formed the basis for the anti-invasion defences of the First World War, together with additional fieldworks built at the time. However, the threat of bombardment from aircraft and airships, something not anticipated until a few years before the war, also required a new form of defence.

After a period of Franco-British colonial rivalry that had threatened to spill over into war (not least during the Fashoda Incident of 1898), the conclusion of the Entente Cordiale in 1904 led to greatly improved relations between Britain and France. Germany, with its programme of naval expansion, was seen as a more likely future enemy and invader. At the same time, the idea gained ground in the Cabinet that invasion was basically a naval problem and preventable by existing British naval resources; this was believed with such confidence that by 1906 the London Defence Scheme was abolished. Yet, when war came in 1914, naval optimism evaporated, and the Admiralty conceded that the fleet could no longer guarantee protection against invasion. Not only did the threat of bombardment of the coast from surface warships have to be met, but vessels in anchorages and harbours now also faced undersea attack from torpedo-firing submarines (a submarine attacked Dover harbour in 1914). There was also the new threat of attack from the air by airships and bombers – and poison gas, as used on the Western Front from 1915, also had to be taken into consideration as a possible invasion weapon.

Fletcher Battery, armed with heavy breech-loaders
Royal Engineers Museum

Defence against attack from the sea

For seaward defence, the batteries of breech-loading guns built between 1895 and 1905 were supplemented with additional temporary gun positions, entrenchments and pillboxes to defend the smaller harbours and possible landing beaches. New works from World War I have left fewer traces than those of World War II, but an important surviving one is Fletcher Battery, for two 9.2-in. (23.4 cm) long-range guns, which was built in 1917 not far from Warden Point on the Isle of Sheppey. This also exhibits an unusual form of double circular pillbox.

A standing naval force defended the estuaries of both the Thames and the Medway. In the Thames, Coalhouse and Cliffe Forts had already superseded the inner line at Gravesend and Tilbury (Shornemead was no longer armed), and the only new development was the building of two gun emplacements on the roof of Cliffe Fort. In the Medway, the offshore Grain Tower was encircled with heavy steel chain to anchor a boom defence stretching across to Sheerness (there was a fixed timber section between the tower and the beach at Grain). This chain and one of two emplacements for quick-firing guns added to the tower roof may still be seen. Some of the wartime additions to the defences at Sheerness have vanished, but two Martello-like concrete gun towers built on the North Lines shortly before 1914 are

Germany, with its programme of naval expansion, was seen as a more likely future enemy and invader.

Fletcher Battery today
Kent County Council

Infantry pillbox near Newington
Victor Smith

Martello Battery at Sheerness
James Chapelard

prominent. Further upstream earthen redoubts, block houses and pillboxes defended the naval dockyard at Chatham and the armament depots at Lodge Hill and Chattenden.

Huge minefields were laid across the English Channel. Dover became the base for the Dover Patrol, which operated in the Channel, and as a defensive measure the western entrance to the harbour was obstructed by blockships. An Admiralty lookout and Port War Signal Station was built above an earlier fire command post at Dover Castle. There was also a scheme for siting a line of concrete gun towers across the Dover Strait, with submarine nets strung out between them. The war ended before this could be implemented, but one of two towers built was towed into a position off the Isle of Wight to become the Nab Tower lighthouse, which exists to this day.

Machine gun position, forming part of the anti-invasion defences
Royal Engineers Museum

Land fronts

An invading army would have been a predominantly infantry force, with
horse-drawn artillery and some motorised transport. It might have aircraft
and (after 1917) a small number of tanks in support. To meet this, a screen
of local (regular and volunteer) forces was to defend against the initial
phases of an invasion, while a large strategic reserve would be held in
readiness to deliver a hoped-for knock-out blow. Defensive trenched stop
lines were built across likely axes of advance from the coast to London, and
some traces of these survive. A major stop line between the Swale and the
country just to the north of Maidstone has left a few traces of trenches in
woodland, together with several concrete pillboxes in fields east of
Newington. A line of four pairs of 6-inch (152 mm) gun emplacements
between Upchurch and Boxley has left evidence at Gore Farm and Matts
Hill, and there are possible traces of trenches on Box Hill. Other
entrenchments joining the Chatham ring forts and connecting them to the
London Mobilisation Centres via a line from Halling to Knockholt formed the
reactivated London Defence Positions but these appear to have left no traces.

Dover also became a vast entrenched camp defended with fieldworks on the
encircling hills. These were added to in 1916 but have left few certain traces,
although there is a circular pillbox from this period at Fort Burgoyne.

Airship sheds at Kingsnorth,
near Hoo
Fleet Air Arm Museum

Defence against air attack

Air raids occurred as early as 1914, initially from Zeppelin airships, but
became more serious with the Gotha bomber raids in 1917, in which London,
Sheerness, Folkestone, Herne Bay and other Kentish towns were bombed.
Defence against air attack involved a combination of anti-aircraft guns and
fighter interceptors. Both were supported by an organisation of ground
observers, to spot and report sightings of enemy aircraft, supplemented by
new methods of acoustic detection in the form of both mobile sound locators
and fixed concrete sound mirrors, such as those built at Fan Bay, Dover, Joss
Gap near North Foreland, and inland at Binbury Manor and London. Air
defence concentrated on the protection of London and the naval and
industrial facilities on the Thames and Medway and at Dover.

Fighters operated from several airfields. These included Eastchurch,
Detling, Manston and Dover, plus more than a dozen other airfields and
landing grounds. There were also seaplane bases at Grain and Dover, and
airship stations at Capel-le-Ferne, Godmersham and Grain carried out coastal
patrols (Grain was more important as a manufacturing centre for airships).
By 1918 there were more than 20 airfields, seaplane bases and airship
stations in Kent, although few meaningful remains of their buildings are left.

By 1917, 200 anti-aircraft guns and 300 searchlights ringed London, with an
outer zone of fighter defence consisting of 150 aircraft, and 27 anti-aircraft
guns. Some 38 searchlights were positioned at Dover, and there was similar
protection for naval facilities in the Medway, at Sheerness and Chatham (an
emplacement survives at Chatham Lines). Several anti-aircraft guns were
mounted to protect the ammunition depots at Lodge Hill (where there are
examples of gun emplacements from the beginning of the war) and
Chattenden. By the end of the war recently developed radio communications
made it possible to co-ordinate interceptor fighters and gun defences, and
height-observation, range-finding and gun-control techniques had also
evolved, and barrage balloons were being used to deter enemy raiders.

Much effort and money was spent on home defence, on the reasonable
assumption that the Germans intended to invade. However, despite
contemporary fears of this, there is little to suggest that the German General
Staff seriously considered invasion after 1916; trench warfare in France and
Belgium absorbed their army's energies. The last time that Germany
challenged British naval supremacy was at the Battle of Jutland in 1916, but
as late as 1918 anxiety arising from the German Ludendorff offensive caused
extra field artillery to be moved to the stop lines in Kent.

Air Defence in the Interwar Years

Early warning
Airfield expansion

12

Germany, with its programme of naval expansion, was seen as a more likely future enemy and invader.

A formation of interwar Hawker
Fury interceptors flying over the
south of England

After World War I the absence of an identifiable enemy initially produced uncertainty about priorities for home defence. After a period of disarmament, the need to achieve a balance of air power with France evolved as a strategic requirement. By the mid-1930s, however, defensive preparations were focusing on Germany as the potential enemy, and on the perceived likelihood of large-scale German air bombardment of Britain in a future war.

In 1919 a European threat did not seem likely in the near future. Consequently, government economies led to defences being reduced. Coastal artillery was retained, though for some years its technology marked time, and permanent defence of land fronts was given up; by 1920 anti-aircraft gun defence was virtually disbanded, and fighter defence reduced to a tiny fraction of its wartime strength. Within a few years, though, efforts were being made to rebuild the air defences, with the protection of London and the south-east the priority. The only power then able to mount an attack was France, so the Royal Air Force was to be enlarged and updated to achieve parity with the projected expansion of the French air force.

The likelihood of a devastating air-bombing offensive in a future war most engaged the attention of home defence planners. As before, a 'layered' scheme of air defence for London was devised consisting of an inner gun zone, fronted by a fighter defence zone and, an outer artillery zone, with observers to warn of incoming aircraft.

The 200ft long sound mirror at Greatstone
Kent County Council

Early warning

The acoustic location methods pioneered during World War I for detecting enemy aircraft at distance, so that fighter interceptors could be launched and anti-aircraft batteries brought to readiness, continued to be used. Many of the locating instruments were mobile units, but considerable investment went into building more fixed concrete mirrors, like those which had been pioneered during World War I; a concave surface received distant engine noise, which was focused on a collector in the form of an ear trumpet or microphone. By swinging the collector to the position in which it best received the aircraft sound, the angle to the target could be estimated. Correlating the angles from two or more mirrors gave a more precise estimate of range and height that could be telephoned to a control room, and fighters could be scrambled from the nearest airfield to intercept the raiders.

In 1924–5 two lines of experimental vertical-searching disc mirrors were established parallel to the coast to report aircraft flying directly overhead. These were succeeded by three types of permanent concrete sound mirror (bowl, dished-slab and strip types) built between the early 1920s and early 1930s in coastal locations: at Greatstone-on-Sea on Romney Marsh(3), Hythe (2), Abbots Cliff (1), Dover (1) and Warden Point on Sheppey (1). To complete an early-warning chain, others were planned for Grain, Swalecliffe, Reculver and elsewhere but were not constructed. Three sound mirrors remain at Greatstone (bowl, slab and strip), along with two at Hythe (bowl and slab, the latter toppled over) and the slab mirror at Abbot's Cliff.

The 30ft diameter sound mirror at Hythe
Victor Smith

The 30ft and 20ft diameter mirrors at Greatstone
Kent County Council

Airfield expansion

After 1935 the air defences were enlarged and extended northwards to Teesside to meet the growing German threat. This incorporated a major expansion of airfield construction that resulted in 89 new or modernised air bases across the country. In Kent the latter focused in varying degrees on Hawkinge, Biggin Hill, Detling, Lympne and later West Malling. The fine neo-Georgian Officer's Mess at Biggin Hill embodies a distinctive architectural form of this period. In addition there was a programme to greatly increase the number of anti-aircraft guns and sites to fulfil the new requirements.

Then came the Munich Crisis of 1938 and, a year later, the outbreak of World War II.

World War II

Air defence
Civil protection against air attack
Coastal defence against raids and invasion
Inland defences against invasion

13

At the outbreak of war in 1939 invasion was not an immediate threat. Allied forces on the continent were in position and expected to be able to deter a German advance west. The main threat to Britain was seen as attack from the air, the potential destructiveness of which had been graphically illustrated during the Spanish Civil War (1936–9). Not until 1940, after Franco-British forces on the continent had been defeated, 300,000 troops had been evacuated from Dunkirk's beaches and Germany controlled the coast of Europe from Norway to the Pyrenees, was an invasion seen as likely –with the German air attacks during the Battle of Britain as its preliminary phase.

Air defence

As a result of the expansion since 1935, air defence was now more national in scope and concentrated upon protecting military and naval assets, ports, industrial centres and key urban areas. In the south-east it was again based on successive zonal layers of defence centred on London. Long-range early warning of approaching aircraft was provided by the new technology of radar (Radio Direction And Ranging), developed shortly before the outbreak of war, which was deployed in a screen of stations known as the Chain Home system. This was supplemented with visual spotting by ground observers. Remnants survive in the steel radar towers at Swingate, near Dover, and Dunkirk, near Canterbury, where there are also extensive ground structures; a surviving ground observation post at Hamstreet is thought to date from World War II.

The outbreak of war brought further, frenetic expansion of the number of airfields and advance and emergency landing grounds. The more important fighter interceptors bases in Kent were Manston, Hawkinge, Detling, Lympne, Biggin Hill and Gravesend, which came into their own during the Battle of Britain in the Summer and Autumn of 1940, and West Malling which became fully operational later. These were grass fields with a range of structures: control tower, hangars, administrative and living accommodation. There are varying survivals at these sites, including a fine control tower at West Malling. There are also remains of dispersed accommodation sites at Hawkinge and Gravesend. The more important and/or vulnerable airfields

The towers of the Swingate radar station near Dover
James Chapelard

Pillbox at Folkestone
Kent County Council

The main threat to
Britain was seen as
attack from the air

Air defences in Kent

Symbol	Meaning
/\/	Sector Boundary
×	Sector HQ
⌐	ROC HQ
⚡	Radar Station
✛	Main Airfields

were also protected by pillboxes and other defences. In addition, false or 'decoy' airfields were established to deceive German pilots into bombing them, and a good example of a control building for one of these is on Cliffe Marshes.

All arms of air defence were linked into a command infrastructure, which gathered information on the threat and took decisions on how to use available defensive resources. Anti-aircraft guns were the new 3.7-in. (94-mm) and 4.5-in. (114-mm) calibres, which had succeeded the 3-in. (76-mm) gun of World War I (some of which were still in use, including, for a time, those on Dover's seafront). They were mostly mounted in groups of four in emplacements, usually consisting of octagonal blast

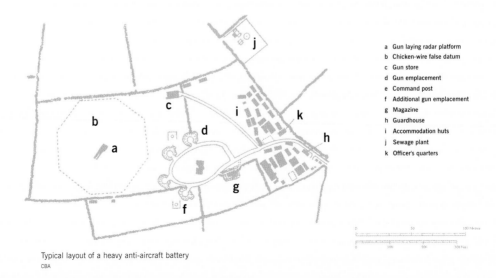

a Gun laying radar platform
b Chicken-wire false datum
c Gun store
d Gun emplacement
e Command post
f Additional gun emplacement
g Magazine
h Guardhouse
i Accommodation huts
j Sewage plant
k Officer's quarters

Typical layout of a heavy anti-aircraft battery
CBA

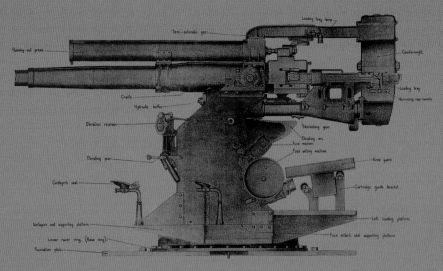

A 3.7-in gun, the mainstay of the British anti-aircraft gun defence
War Office

walls, with ready-use ammunition lockers replenished from on-site magazines. The guns were controlled from a command post, near the centre or rear of the emplacements, which had optical height- and range-finders linked to predictors. Repeated height and range observations enabled the predictors to plot an enemy aircraft's course and speed and generate co-ordinates for the guns to use in firing at their moving targets.

Many batteries also had their own gun-laying radar. Later, greater automation of gun operation became possible with the introduction of the 5.25-in. (133-mm) gun towards the end of the war. Lighter weapons, such as the 40-mm Bofors gun and machine-guns, were used for local defence of airfields and many other vulnerable targets.

In the Thames estuary innovative concrete offshore forts were built

There were also rocket batteries for salvo-firing at formations of aircraft, and tethered barrage balloons were used to create aerial obstacles. Although fixed sound locators had been abandoned, mobile units were still assigned to batteries, and searchlights were provided for night firing, though their sites have left few traces.

Anti-aircraft gun sites may be seen at such places as Dover (Wanstone Farm and Farthingloe), Iwade, Sheppey, Fort Borstal, Cobham and Erith. Fort Luton at Chatham was brought back into use as an Anti-Aircraft Operations Room. Among the emplacements for lighter guns for local defence, individual gun towers survive at West Malling airfield and the Dunkirk radar station, as well as emplacements at Dover Castle. In the Thames estuary innovative concrete offshore forts were built at Northfleet and towed downstream for siting on the river bed, to prevent mining of the waterway and to extend radar cover. Several of them are visible from the coast.

In 1944, under the Diver scheme, many of the guns in Kent were moved to form a screen of fire along the south coast to counteract the new V1 flying bombs, and the offshore forts in the Thames were included in a subsidiary scheme called the Diver Box. There was no defence, however, against an incoming V2 rocket travelling at supersonic speed. V1 launching sites

Imperial War Museum

A coastal defence gun on the roof of Garrison Point Fort at Sheerness

may be seen behind Cherbourg, a V2 manufacturing site at Eperlecques (bombed by the Allies) and an intended launching site at Wizernes (unfinished). Remnants of a V3 'supergun' site, intended for the bombardment of London, are at Mimoyecques near Cap Gris Nez.

One of the anti-aircraft forts in the Thames Estuary

Frank Turner

Restoration: a Bofors light anti-aircraft gun at Dover Castle
James Chapelard

Civil protection against air attack

Planning during the interwar years had correctly foreseen that the scale and intensity of future bombing raids would be vastly greater than in World War I. This led to the creation of an Air Raid Precautions (ARP) organisation for the protection of civil communities, industrial centres and service bases and facilities; large numbers of civilians formed its backbone. Thousands of air-raid shelters were provided (many of which survive as physical reminders), public and other buildings were sandbagged for protection, and emergency water tanks were set up to help fight fires resulting from enemy action. Among the many places in Kent that were bombed, Canterbury suffered particularly from German air raids.

> Thousands of air-raid shelters were provided... buildings were sandbagged for protection

Provision of air-raid shelters was nationally and regionally planned, and allocation for individual families, groups and communities was prioritised according to the risk of attack to the area concerned. In many family gardens earth-covered steel Anderson shelters were erected, or small concrete shelters, while inside some homes Morrison shelters, resembling metal tables, were provided. Community shelters could be either brick structures on the surface or underground shelters, often constructed on the cut-and-cover principle, using prefabricated concrete sections; secure basements of shops or municipal or other public buildings could also be used. Factories, schools and service communities were provided with similar shelters. Civilian shelters were sometimes fitted with primitive air locks to protect their occupants against the possibility of attack with poison gas. Surface shelters survive in many places, not least on school premises, where they have often been reused for educational purposes or storage.

Many cut-and-cover shelters were sealed and forgotten, occasionally to be rediscovered when broken into during redevelopment work. At Ramsgate, Dover, Northfleet, Swanscombe and Chislehurst, existing and extended tunnels in the chalk provided protection for communities, and many of these survive, although only those at Chislehurst are accessible. A remarkable survival at Erith is a major gas decontamination centre in the grounds of Erith Hospital.

Electric or hand-operated air-raid sirens were provided to give warning of an attack. In the civilian community there was also a network of locally based teams of Air Raid Wardens based in small concrete or brick posts. The wardens advised householders on air-raid precautions, enforced black-out restrictions and reported casualties and damage caused by raids to the Civil Defence control centres (often the basements of town halls), from which the deployment of rescue and emergency services was co-ordinated. There are surviving Warden Posts at Dover Priory Station, Gravesend, Gillingham and numerous other places.

Canopied gun emplacement of St Martin's Battery at Dover
Chris Parker

Coastal defence against raids and invasion

As in World War I, the core of the coastal defences at Dover and on the Thames and Medway comprised the batteries built in 1895–1905. After the Dunkirk evacuation it was feared that a German invasion – later codenamed Seelöwe (Sea Lion) – might occur within a few months or even weeks. Frenetic efforts were made to enhance the coastal defences with anti-invasion batteries, especially along vulnerable coastlines between these three main centres. Paradoxically, it was only after 1941, when Germany had turned east to attack Russia, that the defences reached adequacy.

The threat to batteries of dive-bombing and strafing by ground-attack aircraft was countered by building protective canopies over their emplacements or by enclosing the guns in steel shields. Some of the batteries at Dover were canopied, and a good example survives at the rebuilt St Martin's Battery on the Western Heights. The earlier Langdon Battery, on the eastern side of the town, and Citadel Battery on the west, which continued to be used, have left significant remains. The breakwater defences of Dover Harbour were also upgraded, including the mounting of the new twin six-pounder guns, which had an extremely rapid rate of fire and could engage both surface and air targets. These additions have been largely demolished, though a few traces are left, and some contemporary murals survive in a barrack room. Dover continued to have a key role in the defence of the Dover Strait and Royal Navy warships were a frequent sight in the harbour which gained a blockhouse-like pen for motor torpedo boats; a command-and-control centre was sited in tunnels below the Castle, and from here Vice-Admiral Sir Bertram Ramsay planned and directed Operation Dynamo, the evacuation of Dunkirk. These tunnels are now a major heritage site.

To the north and south of Dover, batteries were sited along the coast both to defend against invasion and to deny enemy shipping the use of the Channel. The more important batteries were supplied with gun-laying

Underground telephone exchange at Dover Castle
Victor Smith

Anti-aircraft operations rooms beneath Dover Castle
Victor Smith

'Winnie', one of the giant long-range guns near Dover
Imperial War Museum

radar, which extended their ability to fire at long range, especially in poor visibility. Sometimes the use of guns on the English coast provoked the longer-range German guns in France into firing, particularly on Dover but also on Folkestone and other south-coast locations.

North of Dover are remains of the emplacements and magazines of Wanstone Battery, whose two long-range 15-in. (381-mm) guns were nicknamed 'Clem' and 'Jane'. Some traces of the sites of the 14-in. (356-mm) 'Winnie' and 'Pooh' may be seen at the back of St Margaret's at Cliffe, along with signs of the firing spurs for some heavy rail-mounted guns nearby. The South Foreland Battery of four 9.2-in. (234-mm) guns, has also left a few traces on ground to the rear of the lighthouse, and several observation posts for the gun batteries along the cliffs between Fan Bay and St Margaret's at Cliffe may be seen.

South of Dover, Lydden Spout and Hougham Batteries have left slight traces. More significant remains are those of the line of four observation posts on the cliffs above the Samphire Hoe Country Park (from here and Dover Castle the 'Channel Dash' out of Brest by the German battle cruisers Scharnhorst and Gneisenau and the heavy cruiser Prinz Eugen was spotted by radar in February 1942). At Copt Point, Folkestone, a canopied two-gun harbour-defence battery survives, along with its observation post and a post on top of a Martello tower for a controlled offshore minefield. There is also a canopied anti-invasion battery on the ramparts of the Napoleonic Grand Redoubt at Dymchurch. At Littlestone there is an observation post on top of a water tower, probably linked with a previously existing emergency battery. Just outside the county, at the western end of the Royal Military Canal, is the canopied two-gun Pett Level Battery.

In the Thames, at Coalhouse Fort in Essex, are the canopied emplacements of an emergency battery from this period and, close by, a control tower for a river minefield and another tower to provide low-level radar. No traces remain of the emergency batteries established on Canvey Island (Essex) and Shornemead (Kent), or of the boom defence and associated searchlights between the Kentish shore and Canvey Island, but the fixed section of a long boom extending south from Shoeburyness survives. The guns of the Shoeburyness gunnery school could also be pressed into service as anit-invasion weapons. A twin six-pounder battery can be seen on Grain Tower in the Medway, as can a pair of canopied gun emplacements on the North Lines at Sheerness, and an additional third emplacement and magazines at Fletcher Battery along the coastline. Further east at Shellness is a control building for a minefield in the Swale and the remnants of a small coastal battery.

British coastal defences looked unimpressive against the powerful monumentalism of the German Atlantic Wall fortifications along France's Channel coast, but these were built over a longer period. Unlike their British counterparts, there are many places at which to see them: near Calais (the magnificent Batterie Lindemann and the 'cathedral' shelters for rail guns), Point Le Touquet, Cap Gris Nez, near Boulogne, with some traces at Dunkirk and Le Havre.

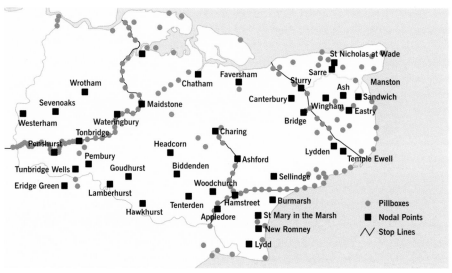

Map of the anti-invasion defences of Kent

Inland defences against invasion

In an invasion, Britain would have faced the blitzkrieg tactics used by the Germans in Poland and France - swift thrusts across country by tanks and partly motorised infantry, supported by devastating dive-bomber attacks ahead of the advance, plus landings behind the British lines by parachute and glider-borne troops to capture airfields and other key points. The preparation of effective defences against such an advance was seriously undermined by the loss of many of the British Army's most modern guns, tanks, vehicles and other equipment in France. General Sir Edmund Ironside, who was appointed Commander-in-Chief of the Home Forces in May 1940, had to do the best he could with the resources actually available at the time.

The strategy initially drawn up was to oppose an invader with a 'coastal crust' of defences, backed by a layered defence inland. The emergency coastal defences already mentioned formed part of the coastal crust, together with pillboxes (of which some remain) and waterline scaffold obstacles and petroleum defences which have left few traces. Inland, the preparations mainly followed an anti-tank strategy. Fortified stop lines were created to contain an advance, and – because it had been noted that in the invasion of France the German armour had advanced primarily along the main roads – it was also decided to defend major intersections (usually in towns) as nodal points or anti-tank islands to slow an enemy advance. The mobile reserve would then concentrate and launch counter-attacks in force.

> General Sir Edmund Ironside had to do the best he could with the resources actually available at the time

Nationally, the largest concentration of such preparations was in the south of the country. In Kent there was an eastern stop line between Dover and Whitstable and a southern line along the bank of the Royal Military Canal, with a spur north to Ashford. Behind these the GHQ Line ran from the bank of the Severn near Bristol to Maidstone, then north to the Thames, resuming on the Essex shore and heading north to Yorkshire and beyond. This was to protect London itself and the vital industrial heartland of the Midlands. There were also three concentric lines of inner defences to protect London itself.

These inland lines were formed of a miscellany of anti-tank gun positions, pillboxes and entrenchments, as well as vehicle obstacles, barriers and minefields – wherever possible utilising existing or natural obstacles such as the River Medway – plus pole-and-wire obstacles to prevent glider landings. The Kentish nodal points (eventually 41 in number) were similarly defended. If retreating, the defending forces were to destroy bridges, railways and roads ahead of the German advance, leaving behind sabotage units to harry the invaders from behind (two secret hides for such units survive on Romney Marsh). Under General Sir Alan Brooke, who succeeded Ironside in July 1940, there was greater emphasis on nodal points as tactical pivots for a more mobile and aggressive defence, described by General Montgomery as requiring '100% binge'.

Firing point for a controlled minefield in the Swale Estuary
Victor Smith

Anti-tank blockhouse covering the Teston Bridge over the Medway
Victor Smith

Anti-tank obstacle at Chartham
James Chapelard

Rifle and machine-gun pillboxes and anti-tank blockhouses have survived in fair numbers. A line of 'coastal crust' pillboxes may be seen on the crest overlooking Folkestone, along the Royal Military Canal and, inland, those of the GHQ Line along the left bank of the Medway and across the Hoo Peninsula via Lodge Hill, with a subsidiary line between Allhallows and High Halstow. One pillbox has been preserved as a village feature at Hamstreet. Good examples of anti-tank blockhouses are at Hoo St Werburgh, Chatham Lines, Adisham, Aylesford, Yalding, Teston and Ensfield Bridge. Airfields with pillboxes may be seen at Hawkinge, West Malling and Detling, which also had Picket Hamilton retractable forts - small circular concrete pillboxes which were sunk into the ground, with their tops flush with the ground, for free movement of aircraft, but which could be raised to defend against ground attack. A few anti-aircraft batteries were also provided with pillboxes, for example those on Erith Marshes. Dover has a network of pillboxes, and others may be seen at a variety of locations. There is an impressive example of a nodal point at Penshurst and remains of another at Tonbridge.

Anti-tank obstacles could be linear ditches or lines of concrete blocks: rectangular cubes, pyramid-shaped 'pimples' or solid cylinders. The ditches protected swathes of country; the concrete structures were deployed across roads, in front of bridges, whether along stop lines or nodal points, along beaches or in the countryside. The ditches have mainly been filled in, but an impressive line of pimples survives at Grain, with others at Strood, Chatham, Graveney, Dover Castle, Bekesbourne and elsewhere. At Walmer there are concrete and steel anti-tank obstacles.

Pillboxes and blocks were often deployed together to channel an enemy into a minefield or to slow him down so that heavy defensive weapons, both within the pillboxes and in other positions, could be brought to bear. These included concealed anti-tank guns or the Blacker Bombard, which fired a projectile with a high-explosive soft head. These were mounted on a concrete dome-headed cylinder with a central stainless steel pivot. Good examples of these may be seen at Citadel Battery, Dover, near Fort Amherst and at Grain Fort. In addition, there were 'fougasse' explosive and flame defences at bridges and key points, but these have left few traces.

As the war turned in the Allies' favour, defence against invasion lost its earlier immediacy, and even before D-Day in June 1944 some home defences were transferred to a less active 'care and maintenance' status. Nonetheless, within two years of the end of World War II in 1945, political circumstances and military technology had again combined to present a fresh set of challenges for the defence of Britain.

The Cold War

Measures against air attack
Civil Defence

14

Soon after World War II the relationship between wartime 'allies of convenience' deteriorated into a tense, armed stand-off between the power blocs of 'Western democracy' and Soviet communism – embodied in the opposing military alliances of the North Atlantic Treaty Organization (NATO) and the

Soon labelled the 'Cold War', this state of tension was to dominate international relations for 45 years.

Warsaw Pact. Soon labelled the 'Cold War', this state of tension was to dominate international relations for 45 years. Since both blocs possessed weapons of mass destruction (primarily nuclear), there was the likelihood of death and destruction on an unprecedented scale if hostilities broke out. This produced new challenges for military and civil defence planners.

In the event of war with the Soviet Union or the Warsaw Pact, Britain and other NATO countries faced conventional or nuclear bombing or missile attacks against military, industrial and infrastructure targets as well as urban centres;

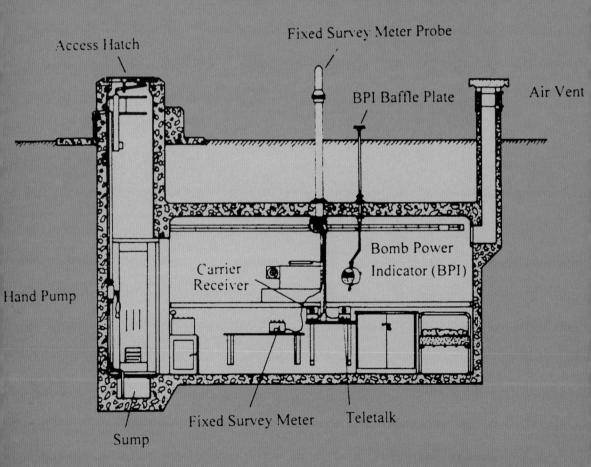

Royal Observer Corps radiation monitoring post
Council for British Archaeology

The Cold War

the use of chemical and biological weapons was also possible. It was assumed officially that war would begin with a conventional phase before escalating to the use of weapons of mass destruction. Kent possessed a variety of valid targets – naval bases, power stations, railway junctions, oil refineries and docks – and was also at risk on account of its infrastructure of ports, roads and railways (which could be used for moving allied troops sent to reinforce the defence against a Soviet land offensive across the continent). There was a protected port HQ for the Royal Navy Auxiliary Service in the magazines of Garrison Point Fort at Sheerness.

Entrance to the underground ROC Group HQ at Maidstone
Victor Smith

Measures against air attack

Coastal defences had continued for a time after World War II and were put on alert during the Korean War (1951–3), when a Soviet attack was feared. Despite proposals to deploy new guns in twin turrets, though, this old technology was overtaken by vulnerability to ground-attack jets, and in 1956 coastal artillery was discontinued in favour of using jet fighter-bombers against invading forces.

   Air attack, rather than invasion, was seen as the greater threat. Defences now had to cope with the fast jets that were supplementing and succeeding earlier, slower piston-engined aircraft. As in the two World Wars, the detection and interception of incoming bombers was crucial. Warning of an air attack was to be given to the civil population by air-raid siren and radio.

Initially, the World War II combination of ground observers and radar was used to plot air attacks (one of the new post-war 'Orlit' posts for the Royal Observer Corps may be seen at Brookland). Information from observers was telephoned to the Group HQ – initially in Beckenham, and subsequently at Ashmore House in Maidstone (still extant), where it had been in World War II – for processing. World War II radars continued in service into the post-war period, but new ROTOR radar stations with underground control centres were established in the early 1950s at Sandwich and St Margaret's at Cliffe; by the 1960s, though, radar detection had taken over completely.

As before, active air defence involved a combination of fighter interceptors and anti-aircraft guns. In Kent, fighters were based at Manston, West Malling and Biggin Hill. Traces of structures used during this period survive at all three sites. Gun defence of the country was divided into zones, of which one was London and the south-east. Protected Gun Operations Rooms co-ordinated the various batteries, one of which (no longer existing) was at Fort Bridgewoods at Chatham. One new gun battery is said to have been built on the Isle of Sheppey, and its emplacements survive. However, faster, higher-performance aircraft rapidly

Entrance to the underground Civil Defence Control Centre at Gravesend
Victor Smith

An anti-aircraft battery at Capel Farm on Sheppey
Kent County Council

outclassed gun defence, so by 1956 guns were discontinued in favour of
air-defence fighters and ground-to-air missiles, though a scheme to deploy
a screen of air-defence missiles along the coast was not taken forward.
Then in the 1960s, however, defensive air power was redeployed from the
south of England to bases in the north-east. These, and NATO airfields on
the continent, now, in effect, provided defence for Kent at a distance.

From the mid-1960s long-range strategic missiles posed an
insurmountable threat. Warsaw Pact attacks with such weapons were seen
as preventable only through the deterrent value of retaliation from similar
NATO missiles sited elsewhere, including those carried in submarines.

The traditional naval presence in the county gradually disappeared after
the Second World War, beginning with the cessation of activity at Dover,
then at Sheerness, and ending with the closure of Chatham Dockyard in
the 1980s.

Civil Defence

Civil Defence used a frame of reference from World War II. Under a
bunkered headquarters built at Tunbridge Wells in 1951, there was a
county control centre at Springfield and a network of local control centres
across the county, linked to local Air Raid Wardens' posts. These were
mainly re-used World War II buildings. The Wardens' posts were to report
to the control centres the extent of casualties and damage so that the
rescue services' efforts could be co-ordinated. At Springfield traces of the
county control survive, together with all of its adjacent successor dating
from 1964, and several local civil defence control centres are extant (the
best example is at Gravesend), as are a number of Wardens' posts in
various locations. Essential services – such as telecommunications,
electricity, water and gas – also had their own protected control rooms.

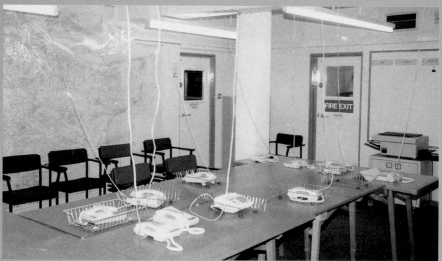

Control room of the County Emergency Centre at Springfield in 1999
Victor Smith

Part of the Regional Seat of Government under Dover Castle
in 1997
English Heritage

With the exception of
the retention of several
military depots, the
last vestiges of military,
naval and civil defence
had ceased to exist

There was, for example, a protected war telephone exchange at Margate.

In the 1950s and 1960s the likely effects of radioactive fallout became a
key concern, and the Royal Observer Corps was given the new role of
monitoring the pattern of nuclear bursts and the spread of radiation from
a network of underground posts across the country; these reported to the
new bunkered Group headquarters built in 1960 next to Ashmore House in
Maidstone. This still survives, and so do a number of the posts, with good
examples at Westerham, Hoo St Werburgh, Manston and Folkestone.

A Regional Seat of Government, established in 1962 in lined chalk
tunnels under Dover Castle, survives. Its facilities were transferred to
Crowborough in 1984.

Civil Defence ceased in 1968, although local authorities were required to
maintain an infrastructure of control centres. However, from the end of
the1980s, as part of the 'peace dividend' following the ending of the Cold
War, the remnants of the civil defence infrastructure began to be
dismantled, and the Royal Observer Corps was abolished in 1991. By the
mid-1990s local authorities were no longer required to maintain war plans.

With the exception of the retention of several military depots, the last
vestiges of military, naval and civil defence had ceased to exist.

Gazetteer

Most artillery defences down to 1900 are included. Because of the great number of World War 2 and other 20th century sites, a selection of examples from their main categories has been given. Some sites have repeat entries to reflect significant later developments or additions.

• This gazetteer is not a definitive statement of right of access. This should be checked beforehand. Hazards may exist at some sites and personal care for safety should be exercised when visiting.

• Opening hours and admission fees, where in operation, are not given because these are subject to revision.

Key

EH English Heritage site

NT National Trust site

OA Open access

IA Informal access possible

VO View from the outside

OR Open regularly

OO Open occasionally

OH Open hardly ever, or by appointment

FP Formal parking, whether part of the site or unconnected with it but within walking distance

IP Informal parking, whether at the site or nearby

Chapter 1 - Castles and Cannon

Canterbury City Walls, Canterbury (TR 146578) OA (walls) OR (Westgate) FP (both)
Late 14th century circuit of stone walls on the line of earlier Roman defences. Seventeen wall towers (many with key-hole shaped gun ports) survive on the east side of the city and may be seen from The Canterbury Trail. The West Gate displays 18 gun ports on three levels and contains a museum.

Cooling Castle, Cooling (TQ 754759) VO
Late 14th century residential castle, consisting of two enclosed courtyards with gatehouses and corner towers. One of the earliest examples of a castle designed with artillery defence in mind. Its towers and gatehouses display key-hole and circular gun loops. The twin-towered gatehouse to the outer enclosure, visible from a nearby road, has circular loops.

Hever Castle, Hever (TQ 478452) OR FP
A rectangular 15th century moated castle, with key-hole shaped gun loops in the gatehouse.

Queenborough Castle, Queenborough (TQ 913722) OA IP
Former concentric castle, built 1361-77 and provided with firearms. Demolished in the 1640s. Now only a low mound next to Queenborough railway station. Buried remains of walls are sometimes visible as parched areas of grass during very dry weather.

Sandwich Town Defences, Sandwich (TQ 330582) OA FP
An almost complete circuit of 15th century town defences, accessible along the Sandwich Trail.
It consists of a well-defined earthen bank (at places surviving to a height of 7m.) and a ditch. Fishergate (1384 with 16th century addition) spans a small lane leading into the town.

Chapter 2 - Henry VIII's New Fortifications

Deal Castle, Deal (TR377522) EH OR FP
The largest of Henry VIII's coastal forts, built in 1539-40 and the centrepiece of 'the three castles which keep the Downs'. A central circular tower rises above six small attached rounded bastions, separated from an outer ring of six larger bastions by a courtyard, the whole being surrounded by a dry ditch. Many defensive features and areas of former domestic occupation are accessible to visitors.

Dover Castle, Dover (TR 324419) EH OR FP
A small gun platform, possibly of Henrician date, juts out into the west castle ditch near the cliff edge. It is visible from the bridge into Canon's Gate.

Gravesend Blockhouse, Gravesend (TQ 649744) VO FP
One of five artillery blockhouses built in 1539/40 to defend the river route to London and the only one of them exposed to view. Part of the brick curved front of the building and blocked gun ports can be seen from a riverside path.

Kingsgate Folly Fort, Kingsgate (TR 395709) VO
Cliff-top folly fort built in the 18th century, apparently in imitation of the architectural forms of Walmer and Sandown Castles.

Sandgate Castle, Sandgate (TQ 208353) VO FP
Built by Henry VIII to defend the coastal road and the adjoining beach. A stone structure with a central gun tower surrounded by a triangle of three bastions linked by an outwardly curving curtain wall. A matching outer wall has a defensible gatehouse to landward. The central tower was converted to a Martello Tower during the Napoleonic Wars.

Sandown Castle, Sandown (TR 375544) OA FP
One of the three Downs castles. Similar design to Walmer Castle. Its site and the encased residue of some buried remains are marked by an information panel.

Walmer Castle, Walmer (TR 377501) EH OR FP
The southernmost of 'The three castles which keep the Downs', built in 1539/40. Similar to Deal Castle, but simpler, having just one level of four bastions around its central tower. Altered at several points in the 18th and 19th centuries for use as a residence for the Lord Warden of the Cinque Ports. Contains good examples of gun ports, a collection of guns and a display of gardens

Chapter 3 - Angular Bastions and the Spanish Armada

Milton Blockhouse, Gravesend (TQ 655723) VO FP
The site of another of the Thames blockhouses, with an additional early angular bastion (1545-7) which has been archaeologically excavated. Its backfilled remains have been marked as an outline on the surface of the ground.

Upnor Castle, Upnor (TQ 758706) EH OR FP
Built in 1559 (and enlarged in 1599-1601) to protect the naval anchorage in Chatham Reach. A large angular bastion with embrasures projects into the river, with a towered barrack range behind on the riverbank. To the rear of the barrack is a courtyard enclosed by a now partly filled ditch and a wall, which linked the north and south towers with a square gatehouse. Displays and exhibits.

Chapter 4 - The Seventeenth Century: Peace and War

Archcliffe Fort, Dover (TR 315402) OR (shop) FP (shop)
Dating from the first few years of the 17th century it defended the entrance and approaches to the old Dover Harbour. Seaward-facing gun lines joined with a curtain wall and two bastions facing the land. Two landward sides and the bastions survive, together with the entrance arch and part of the ditch. Internally are some later barrack buildings, occupied by the Emmaus Community. One is used as a shop. Access to this provides some good views of the inside of the fort.

Cockham Wood Fort, Hoo St. Werburgh (TQ 777712) IA
Built between 1668-early 70s as part of Bernard de Gomme's strengthening of the Medway defences. It consisted of two levels of gun emplacements stepped into the riverside slope, within rectangular earthwork rampart and ditch. There was a brick tower in the centre of the rear rampart. The outline of the fort survives, its most prominent feature being the brick revetment to the lower battery, accessible from a riverside footpath.

De Gomme's Sheerness Defences, Sheerness (TQ 909756) VO FP
Built at the same date as Cockham Wood Fort to enclose and defend the new Sheerness dockyard. There is a surviving stretch of wall and the stone base of a guerite or sentry box, on its corner, visible from the western end of the esplanade.

Chapter 5 - The Eighteenth Century: Reaction to Continental Wars

Chatham Lines, Chatham (TQ 759683-771695) VO
Built from 1755 to defend Chatham Dockyard against attack from the land. They consisted of an earthen bastioned line (later brick encased and extended) 2.4 km long, with return lines to the river bank at either end. Mainly in closed military areas, but with stretches visible on either side of Brompton Road, especially to the south in a housing estate and within Fort Amherst.

Dover Castle, Dover (TR 324419) EH OR FP
Within the Castle is a range of new barracks built around the keep in 1745. Elsewhere within the castle are modifications c.1755-6 of the medieval walls and towers as part of the modernisation of the site for artillery defence.

Motes Bulwark, Dover (TR 325415) EH VO IP
Low level semi-circular battery built at the foot of the Dover Castle Cliffs. Visible from a nearby footpath.

Sheerness Land Defences (TQ 916751) OA IA FP
Advanced bastioned line built in the 1780s- 90s in rear of the expanding Sheerness Dockyard which was outgrowing the earlier de Gomme defences. A remnant survives in the form of a pair of bastions, a joining rampart and part of a ravelin, close to the Tesco Supermarket.

Chapter 6 - The French Revolutionary and Napoleonic Wars

Delce Tower, Rochester (TQ 747678) OA
Slight remains of this gun-tower (c. 1810) may be seen at the top of a bank on the eastern side of Delce Road.

Dover Castle, Dover (TR 324419)
EH OR FP
Between 1794 and 1805 the Castle's eastern defences were massively strengthened by an earthwork built against the medieval wall, by the widening and deepening of its ditch, and by the construction of four major detached works: Horseshoe, Hudson's, East demi and East Arrow Bastions. These, with additions to the spur work and casemates built at Canon's gate, are visible in varying degrees as part of the usual castle tour.

Drop Redoubt, Dover (TR315411)
VO FP
Part of the Western Heights defences. It evolved from a fieldwork begun at the end of the 1780s, and was rebuilt in the Napoleonic Wars. The plan is pentagonal with later caponiers on four of the angles. Within the redoubt are gun positions and casemated barracks.

Dungeness Battery No. 1,
Dungeness (TR088186) IA IP
Built in the mid-1790s to defend the adjacent landing beaches and offshore anchorage. Its arc of 5 gun emplacements survives. The V-shaped enclosure to the rear was demolished in the 1970s. The remains are marked with a plaque.

Dungeness Battery No. 2, Lade (TR 083206) IA IP
A more complete example of the same, close to the coastal road. An internal building is in use as residential housing.

Dungeness Redoubt (TR 085172)
IA IP
Same dates as Batteries No.1 and 2 and forming part of the anti-invasion measures of the French Revolutionary Wars. An 11-sided regular polygon formed of a shingle rampart, fronted by a ditch. Reachable from a nearby track.

Fort Amherst, Chatham (TQ 760684) OR FP
The nucleus was the Amherst Redoubt c. 1770 at the southern end of Chatham Lines, to which was added a complex of retrenchments during the Napoleonic Wars. This major visitor attraction displays a hornwork, the Amherst Redoubt, a large brick guardhouse, various batteries, casemated barracks and the barrier ditch, as well as a display of mounted guns.

Fort Clarence, Rochester (TQ 739677) VO
Built by 1812 as part of the outer landward defences to protect Chatham Dockyard. It consists of an arrow-head shaped brick tower set in a 600-m long ditch extending east from the riverbank.

Fort Pitt, Chatham (TQ 750675)
VO IP
A surviving curtain and two bastions of this fort finished in 1819 can be seen in playing fields of the Fort Pitt Secondary School.

Grand Redoubt, Dymchurch (TR 129322) VO IP
One of two 11-gun anti-invasion redoubts on the south coast associated with the Martello Tower system. It was built in 1806 and consists of a circular brick structure with a central parade surrounded by 11 radially placed gun emplacements set over bomb-proof barracks and magazines. The Second World War gun emplacements on its roof can best be seen from the sea wall.

Grand Shaft, Dover (TR 316409)
OR FP
A triple spiral staircase built by 1807 to provide communication between the Western Heights defences and the town of Dover and the harbour.

Martello Towers, Folkestone (TR 240366) OO FP and Dymchurch (TR 101290). OO FP
Built in 1805-8, as part of the defences of the south coast. There were 27 towers in Kent, of which 16 survive. They resemble an upturned flower-pot, having a position for a single gun on the roof, with barracks, magazine and cistern within the body of the tower. The Folkestone and Dymchurch towers are the only ones open to visitors but all of the others can be seen from either the coastal road or, where on the higher ground inland, from other roads and tracks.

Royal Military Canal (TQ 940254 - TR 188348) OA IP/FP
Part of the anti-invasion defences of the Napoleonic Wars, consisting of a rampart with traverses and wet ditch from Shorncliffe to Pett Level in Sussex, cutting off the country behind to an invader. There was a military road behind the rampart. The ditch was also a canal with a towpath along its northern edge. Representative stretches can be seen from public footpaths at Appledore, east of Bridge Farm, at Hythe and elsewhere. WW2 pillboxes are to be seen at some of the traverses. At the Shorncliffe end is a small Napoleonic battery.

Sandwich Bay Battery No. 2, Sandwich (TR 363575) VO FP
One of two batteries built on the shoreline north of Sandown in the 1790s to defend adjacent landing beaches and an offshore anchorage. It is a chevron-shaped battery with the rear closed by a loopholed wall and by buildings to provide barrack accommodation. There are good views of the exterior from the coastal footpath.

Shorncliffe Battery, Shorncliffe (TR 192349) VO FP
Built near the eastern end of the Royal Military Canal in 1804. Visible from the coastal road as a flat bastioned structure with surmounting earthworks.

Shorncliffe Redoubt, Shorncliffe (TR 193353) IA
On the heights overlooking the eastern end of the Royal Military Canal. Built about the same date, surviving as a tree-lined rectangular earthwork with traces of ditch.

Western Heights Defences, Dover (TR 311406) OA (perimeter trail) FP
A large complex of forts and batteries joined by ramparts and ditches, enclosing the end of a prominent hill overlooking the port of Dover from the western side of the Dour Valley. Started in the French Revolutionary and Napoleonic Wars and, after a gap of several decades, finished in the 1850s and 60s.

Chapter 7 - After Waterloo: Forts and Technology

Cliffe Fort, Cliffe (TQ 706767) VO
This river bank site dates from the 1860s and was part of the modernisation of the Thames defences. It consists of an arc of armoured gun casemates for the new rifled muzzle-loaders, with an open battery at the up river end, with the rear closed by a defensible barracks faced in Kentish Rag. There are 20th century gun positions on the roof and the launching bay of an 1890s Brennan Torpedo Station in front of the open battery. The fort can be seen from a riverbank footpath.

Dover Castle, Dover (TR 324419)
EH OR FP (castle in general)
The modernisation of the seaward-facing defences of the castle in the 1850s and 60s is reflected in the surviving Shot Yard and Shoulder of Mutton Batteries on the cliffs and in the addition of, or modification to, caponiers in the castle ditch. Salvin's Officers mess dates from this period.

Fort Burgoyne, Dover (TR 324427) VO
New fort built by 1870 to defend the northern approaches to Dover Castle. Its plan was a flattened chevron, with a large v-shaped earthwork facing south towards the castle, and wing ramparts extending from either flank to two outlying redoubts. In army occupation. Glimpses can be seen from a nearby road.

Fort Darnet, Medway (TQ 806707) VO
Dating from the 1860s, and built on Darnet Ness. This is a circular version of Cliffe Fort, and formed part of the inner defences of the Medway. Its magazines are flooded to their ceilings. It is reachable by boat but is off limits to visitors.

Garrison Point Fort And Seaward Defences, Sheerness (TQ 908756) VO FP
Garrison Point Fort is a two-tier version of Cliffe Fort, built in 1872 to cross its fire with the new defences at Grain. Development and use of the fort since the 1960s has mutilated some of its features, but it still presents as an impressive and monumental structure, enhanced with later roof emplacements, visible from Sheerness's esplanade. Along the latter may also be seen the batteries of the seaward-facing lines.

Grain Fort and Grain Defences, Grain (TQ 890766) OA FP
On the river's edge east of Grain Village, Grain Fort was built in 1867 to cross its fire with the defences at Sheerness and so close the entrance to the Medway. This heptagonal work, originally with a brick keep, survives as an earthwork and ditch only, the former displaying traces of 20th century gun emplacements. There is a sunken way joining the fort to Grain Battery (remains 1000m to the south), together with traces of other later batteries, most within a public open space.

Grain Tower, Grain (TQ 898760) VO
Built offshore in 1855 as part of an enhancement of the defences at the mouth of the Medway. Its granite faced brick structure resembles the upturned flower pot form of the earlier Martello Towers. Three guns were mounted on its roof. The latter is surmounted by the distinctive additions of the period immediately before WW1 and those of the Second World War when a barrack was built on stilts next to the tower. Access is along a hard way from the shore at low tide and is hazardous.

Hoo Fort, Medway (TQ 796703) VO
The same as Fort Darnet but its magazines are dry. It is also reachable by boat but is off-limits to visitors.

New Tavern Fort, Gravesend (TQ 652742) OR FP
This Thames riverside fort, now a public garden, was remodelled in 1868-72 and displays 4 of the 10 open gun emplacements then provided, including one with a rare example of a casemate shield which has been re-armed with a replica gun. Part of the underlying magazine complex has been refurnished.

Queenborough Lines, Sheerness (TQ 909733-937748) OA IP
A mid-19th century addition to the land defence of Sheerness. This 3.3 km long defence consisted of a low earthen rampart fronted by a wide, wet ditch, defended along it length from two short flanks near the centre and by works at its ends. Much of the Lines can be viewed from a footpath.

Shornemead Fort, Shorne
(TQ 692747) OA/IA IP
The same date, purpose and design
as Cliffe Fort, reachable from either
the river wall trail or across Shorne
Marshes. All that survives is the
façade of the river front of gun
emplacements, whose partly
demolished state reveals useful
detail of its construction.

Slough Fort, Allhallows
(TQ 838784) VO
A smaller version of the forts at
Cliffe and Shornemead and built in
1867, to prevent a landing along
the nearby bank of the Thames.
The front was earthed up in the
later 19th century, when wing
batteries were added. The fort is in
use as riding stables.

Western Heights Defences, Dover
(TR 311406) OA (perimeter trail) FP
The final touches to complete these
defences can be seen in the form of
parts of the new Western Outwork,
extensions to the ditch system, the
caponiers added to the Drop
Redoubt and other features, such as
the seaward facing St. Martin's
battery, (largely overwhelmed by
Second World War modernisation).

Chapter 8 - The Chatham Ring Fortress

Fort Borstal, Rochester
(TQ 733664) VO
One of the seven works forming the
Chatham Ring Fortress, finished in
the 1890s. Now a private
residence. On an asymmetrical
plan, it consists of a front rampart
for guns over casemated barracks
and magazines, with a separate rear
rampart covering further casemates,
the whole being surrounded by a
concrete-revetted ditch raked from
counterscarp firing positions. Both
ramparts are surmounted by a
WW2 anti-aircraft battery. A view of
the fort is possible from a
neighbouring road.

Fort Horsted, Gillingham
(TQ 752651) VO
A similar but larger fort on a
chevron plan, now used as the
headquarters of a landscape
gardening company.

Fort Luton, Chatham (TQ 762660)
VO
A smaller version on an
asymmetrical plan and without
counterscarp firing positions.
Now derelict.

Twydall Redoubts, Twydall
(TQ 798686 and 795682) VO
These redoubts were constructed in
1886 and 1888 respectively. The
rampart and ditch of the first
redoubt survives and the casemate
block of the second, next to the
North Kent railway line.

Chapter 9 - Technology Marches On: Breech-Loaders for Coastal Defence

Citadel Battery, Dover
(TR 304403) OA
Self-contained concrete battery for 3
heavy breech-loaders built in 1895,
west of the extremity of the Western
Heights defences. With underlying
magazines. A good example of its
type and reachable along the
Western Heights footpath.

Cliffe Fort Brennan Torpedo Station,
Cliffe (TQ 706767) IA
One of two launching bays for the
wire-guided Brennan Torpedo for
river defence is visible from the river
wall trail in front of Cliffe Fort.

Dover Harbour Breakwater
Defences, Dover (TR 320402-
329399-331402-341409-
340416) VO
To protect the new and vast harbour
of refuge built from 1904.
Consisting of batteries, barracks,
searchlight positions and boom
defences, on the extremity of the
harbour arms and breakwaters.
Although not publicly accessible
they are interesting enough to merit
viewing at a distance through
binoculars.

Dover Turret, Dover (TR 321399)
VO
For the protection of Dover Harbour.
A 700-ton rotating iron turret
mounting two 16-in. (40-cm)
calibre 80 ton rifled muzzle-loading
guns, built in 1878 on the eve of
the breech-loading age. This
impressive structure can be viewed
externally by walking along the
Admiralty Pier.

Langdon Battery, Dover
(TR 338424) VO FP
A self-contained concrete battery for
five breech-loading guns, on the
cliffs east of Dover Castle. Two of its
emplacements have been overbuilt
to receive the structures of the
Dover Strait coastguard station.
Reachable along a footpath.

New Tavern Fort, Gravesend
(TQ 652742) OR FP
An exemplar of the new type of low-
profile concrete battery built in
1904 for two breech-loading guns.
Set in a public garden. With
underlying magazines and ammunition lifts. It has been rearmed with
original guns of the period.

Sheerness Seaward Defences,
Sheerness (TQ 913754) VO FP
Examples of the new gun positions
for breech-loaders may be seen
externally along the length of the
Sheerness esplanade and at
Bartons Point.

South Boom Battery, Burntwick
Island (TQ 868727) VO
Remains of this battery, a
counterpart of the now vanished
North Boom Battery, exist on the
north-east corner of Burntwick
Island. It consists of two gun bases,
machine-gun emplacements,
defence electric light cells and a
barrack building. Though accessible
to boats it is off-limits to visitors,

Chapter 10 - London's Land Defences

Of the three Kentish sites, Halstead
(TQ 499591) is inaccessible within
a Ministry of Defence security area,
Westerham (TQ 435563) is too
mutilated to view and is on private
property and Farningham
(TQ533668) is within a golf course,
not publicly accessible.

Chapter 11 - World War 1

Fletcher Battery, Isle of Sheppey
(TR 003727) IA FP (camp users
only)
Built in 1917 to mount two heavy
guns to fire on the Thames Estuary.
A standard type of battery but with
a WW1 pillbox on its left flank and
a third WW2 gun emplacement on
its right flank. In the middle of a
holiday caravan park.

Lodge Hill Anti-Aircraft Battery,
Chattenden (TQ 758740) VO
A rare example of a First World War
anti-aircraft battery is visible from a
track on MOD land. It consists of
two concrete gun emplacements
and ancillary buildings.

Martello Battery, Sheerness
(TQ 914754) VO FP
A pair of concrete Martello-like
towers (later modified) built in
1913 to mount a breech-loaders on
each. Visible from Sheerness'
esplanade.

Newington Pillboxes, Newington
(TQ 871642 + 864637 +
864637 + 872640) IA
Four examples of pillboxes can be
seen from farm tracks in fields east
of Newington.

Chapter 12 - Air Defence in the Interwar Years

Abbots Cliff Sound Mirror, Dover
(TR 272386) OA
A 20 ft. 'slab type' (1928) on the
side of a coastal footpath.

Greatstone Sound Mirrors,
Greatstone (TR 075213) VO IP
A group of three concrete sound
mirrors built 1927-9 near the edge
of a flooded quarry: 20ft. slab type,
30ft. bowl and a 200ft. strip mirror.
Can be viewed as a group from a
distance over the quarry fence.

Hythe Sound Mirror, Hythe
(TR 139345) OA/IA IP
30ft. bowl mirror (1929) near a
footpath over hillside known as
'The Roughs', overlooking the
Hythe coast.

Chapter 13 - World War II

Adisham Anti-Tank Pillbox,
Adisham (TR 225546) IA
North of Adisham Court, on the
south side of the Canterbury to
Dover railway line.

All Hallows-High Halstow Line Of
Pillboxes (TR 831784-779753)
partly OA and partly IA
Line of 7 pillboxes, 3 of which have
unrestricted access at the All
Hallows end, 3 are close to tracks
and the other is in a private garden.

Bekesbourne Anti-Tank Obstacles,
Bekesbourne (TR 199557) OA
Impressive triple line of pyramidal
anti-tank blocks in a field at the
side of a public footpath.

Chislehurst Caves, Chislehurst
(TQ 433696) OR FP
Pre-existing system of chalk tunnels
used as public air raid shelters.
Alterations made for that purpose
can be seen on the public tour.

Cliffe Airfield Decoy Building, Cliffe
(TQ 729772) IA IP
Control point at the side of a track
for a night decoy airfield on Cliffe
Marshes. Small brick building with
a concrete roof.

Copt Point Battery, Folkestone
(TR 240366) OA FP
One of a number of 'emergency
batteries' built during German
invasion threat of 1940/1. Consists
of 2 gun houses, with overhead
protection against air attack, and
a fire control position on rising
ground behind. A Second World
War control point for an offshore
minefield surmounts the adjacent
Martello Tower.

Court at Street Pillbox, Court at
Street (TR 093354) VO
Pillbox adapted from a c.1895 farm
building. Part of a line of defences
on the escarpment overlooking
Romney Marsh.

Detling Airfield And Defences,
Detling (TQ 813595) VO IA
Remnants of the technical and
domestic area are within an
industrial estate. Combined surface
and AA pillboxes in former landing
grounds are viewable from footpaths.

Dover Castle Command And
Control Centre And Underground
Hospital And Ww2 Defences, Dover
(TR 324419) EH OR FP
Vice-Admiral Sir Bertram Ramsay's
headquarters from which he
planned Operation Dynamo, the
evacuation from Dunkirk, is
displayed. The adjacent wartime
underground hospital has been
refurnished for inspection by visitors.
The pre-war signal station displays
a reinforced concrete roof from this
period. Emplacements for light anti-
aircraft guns are on the eastern
rampart of the outer bailey, with a
radar position on the cliff edge.
Concrete anti-tank pimples are near
the spur and there is an anti-tank
position in the curtain wall of the
castle nearby. Another anti-tank
position is close to Horseshoe Bastion.

Dover Priory Station Air Raid
Wardens Post, Dover (TR 314414)
VO FP
Small rectangular brick structure
with a concrete roof, on the 'down'
side of Dover Priory Station.

Dunkirk Chain Home Radar Station,
near Canterbury (TR 076593)
VO IA
The single remaining tower is a
prominent landscape feature. There
are also a receiving block, pillboxes
and an AA gun tower at the side of
a track in Clay Pits Wood.

Eastry Pillbox, Poison Cross
(TR 311555) VO
On the edge of a fruit orchard, the
pillbox has two levels of loopholes,
the lower one for the Boys
anti-tank rifle.

Ensfield Bridge Pillboxes, Ensfield
(TQ 547454 and 547453) VO
A pair of anti-invasion pillboxes for
the defence of the Ensfield Bridge,
carrying a road over the Medway. A
typical example of bridge defences,
consisting of one anti-tank pillbox
and one machine gun type.

Erith Heavy Anti-Aircraft Battery,
Crayford Marshes (TQ 530773) VO
Four-gun battery, with command
post, outlying pillboxes, air raid
shelter and other structures, on
marshland at the side of Wallhouse
Road.

Erith Hospital Gas Decontamination
Centre, Erith (TQ 506776) OH FP
Bunkered and mounded structure in
the grounds of Erith Hospital, open
to visitors annually.

Farthingloe Heavy Anti-Aircraft
Battery, Dover (TR 296400) VO
A typical 4-gun battery, with
magazine, command post and gun
store, at the side of a track 800-m.
west of the Western Heights
Citadel Battery.

Folkestone Pillboxes (TR192381-
240377) VO
A line of 9 'coastal crust' anti-
invasion pillboxes along the crest of
the hills behind Folkestone. Visible
from West and East Crete Roads.

Frogham Road Block, Frogham (TR
250502) OA
Scars of the sockets for obstacles
can be seen in the mettling of the
Frogham-Wollage Green road where
it crosses a railway line on a bridge.
There are concrete pimples in the
grass on either side of the north end
of the bridge.

Grain Beach Obstacles (TQ
883774-888771) IA FP
Line of concrete anti-tank blocks, 8
deep, from the western extremity of
the esplanade at Grain extending
WNW across marshland to the edge
of the MOD explosive range.

Grand Redoubt, Dymchurch
(TR 129322) VO IP
Seaward-facing WW2 canopied gun
positions and pillboxes may be seen
on the roof of the Napoleonic
redoubt.

Graveney Road Block, Graveney
(TR 063647) IA
A good example of a road block,
consisting of concrete blocks and
circular drums, impeding the way
between water courses in the
Graveney Marshes.

Great Farthingloe Observation
Posts, Dover (TR 289392) NT OA
Line of 4 cliff top observation posts
and ancillary buildings next to the
coastal footpath. These served
nearby Lydden Spout and Hougham
Batteries by observing the English
Channel to detect enemy naval
targets. The cliff is hazardous.

Hamstreet Observer Corps Post,
Hamstreet (TR 006331) OA IP
A brick structure, said to date from
WW2, on the south side of the
B2067 near Hamstreet. It was a
post for observers to search the sky
for enemy aircraft. Within its fenced
enclosure is also an underground
post dating from 1961, from which
to monitor radioactive fallout from a
nuclear attack.

Hawkinge Airfield And Defences,
Hawkinge (TR 211394) IA
(airfield in general) OR FP
(museum)
Survivals of the technical and
domestic areas. Site of the Kent
Battle of Britain Museum. There are
pillboxes (surface and combined
AA) around the airfield perimeter.
Air-raid shelters and a gas
decontamination building from the
airfield's dispersed accommodation
can be seen in Reinden Wood 1.5 km
to the north (TR 216416) OA FP.

Hoo-Lodge Hill Line Of Pillboxes
(TQ 761711-793717-771746-
747737) VO
Over 40 anti-tank and infantry
pillboxes forming part of the GHQ
defence line as it diverges from the
left bank of the Medway across the
Hoo Peninsula to join the right bank
of the Thames. Some are close to
tracks.

Iwade Heavy Anti-Aircraft Battery,
Iwade (TQ 899689) VO IA
On rising ground overlooking the
Swale Estuary, visible to those using
the industrial estate or the
speedway track on the site. It
consists of a gun site with two
groups of emplacements from
different periods of development,
together with a command post,
magazine and barracks.

Manston Airfield, Manston
(TR 335662) VO airfield in
general; museum OR FP
Originally established in WW1, the
airfield saw action in WW2. Its
continued use is both for civil
aviation and for RAF Search and
Rescue. Buildings include the WW1
station HQ, two general service
hangars, early timber barracks, the
control tower and technical
buildings and brick-clad FIDO fuel
tanks. It is the site of the Spitfire
Memorial Museum.

Northfleet Air-Raid Warden's Post,
Northfleet (TR 637735) VO IP
Small rectangular concrete building
in garden of Campbell Arms Public
House.

Offshore Forts, Thames Estuary VO
Several of the two types of army
and naval manned anti-aircraft gun
towers in the Thames estuary are
visible from the North Kent coast
and, at closer quarters, from
excursion vessels which sometimes
sail out to them.

Penshurst Nodal Point, Penshurst
(TQ 526437)
A compact and comprehensible
example of a Nodal Point. At least
12 pillboxes ring Penshurst village.
Most are in pasture or parkland,
and are on public rights of way.

Shellness Minefield Contol Post,
Sheppey (TR 052676) OA FP
Concrete roofed structure used as
an observation and firing point for a
defensive controlled minefield in the
Swale Estuary. On the edge of a
nature reserve and reached by a
footpath.

South Foreland Battery,
St. Margarets at Cliffe
(TR 358436) OA IP
Public open space containing some
traces of this important long range
cross-channel gun site. Next to a
coastal footpath on the cliffs near
the South Foreland Lighthouse is a
twin-celled observation post
providing fire control for the battery.

St. Margaret's Bay Pillbox And
Tunnels (TR 367444) VO FP
Anti-invasion pillbox and wartime
tunnels can be viewed from the
beach car-park.

St. Martin's Battery, Western
Heights, Dover
(TR 314407) OA FP
A good example of an anti-invasion
battery with canopied overhead
protection against air attack. Its 3
emplacements were built over an
1870's battery in 1940. On-site
interpretation.

Swingate Chain Home Radar
Station, Dover (TR 335428) VO
The steel towers make this a
prominent landscape feature. There
are also transmitting/receiving
blocks and close defence pillboxes.

Teston Bridge Pillboxes, Teston
(TQ 710536 and 710535) VO
A pair of anti-invasion pillboxes for
defence of the Teston Bridge carrying a road across the Medway. A
typical example of bridge defence,
consisting of one anti-tank pillbox
and a machine gun type.

Wanstone Battery, St. Margarets at
Cliffe (TR 354429) VO
Important cross-channel gun site for
two heavy long-range guns called,
'Clem' and 'Jane'. On private land,
their mounded magazines are
landscape features.

Warden Point Coast Defence Radar
Station, Sheppey (TR 019725)
OA IP
Concrete structure which has
gradually slid down the eroding clay
cliffs to dive spectacularly into the
beach at the waterline.

West Malling Airfield And Defences,
West Malling (TQ 676562) OA/IA
IP
Accessible from the road system of
the King's Hill Business Park are the
Control Tower and other airfield
buildings, a fixed and a retractable
pillbox and an anti-aircraft gun
tower, air raid shelters and post-war
barracks.

Chapter 14 - The Cold War

Brookland Roc Post, Brookland
(TQ 987254) VO
Two-person prefabricated surface
concrete observation post built on
stilts in 1953. Part of a national
network established to observe
and report the movement of
hostile aircraft.

Copt Point, Folkestone Roc Post,
Folkestone (TR 240366) VO FP
Small underground concrete 3
person bunker (1960s), one of a
national network established for
observers to record the location,
height and power of nuclear burst
and to monitor radioactive fallout.
Its surface features survive within
a public open space next to a
Martello Tower.

Gravesend Civil Defence Control
Centre, Gravesend (TQ 644728)
OH
Rectangular underground bunker
built in 1954 from which to co-
ordinate local rescue and
emergency services in the event of
a nuclear attack. A grassed mound,
with an entrance and exit, as well
as surface features.

Lydd Range Roc Post, Lydd
(TR 025199) VO
Similar to the post at Copt Point but
unusual in being partly above
ground, encased within a shingle
mound.

Maidstone Roc Group Hq,
Maidstone (TQ 750559) VO
Underground HQ bunker with a
surface element, built in 1960 for
No. 1 Group of the Royal Observer
Corps, in which reports from
individual underground posts were
to be received and processed.

Glossary

Barbette - a platform within a fort from which guns may fire over a parapet without an embrasure.

Bastion - a projection from the general outline of a fortress from which the garrison can defend the ground in front of the ramparts by flanking fire. From the mid-16th century generally a four-sided angled projection.

Battery - a place where guns or mortars are mounted.

Blacker bombard - an anti-tank weapon issued to the Home Guard in World War 2 and fired from a fixed position on a concrete drum with a stainless steel spigot in the centre. Also known as a spigot mortar.

Blast wall - a protective wall in front of vulnerable openings to reduce the effect of bomb or shell blast.

Blockhouse - a small detached fort at a strategic point.

Bomb-ketch - a coastal bombardment vessel armed with a mortar.

Boom - a barrier consisting of spars or a chain etc. stretched across a river or harbour mouth to obstruct navigation.

Breech-loader - a gun loaded from the rear or breech end.

Bulwark - an early term for a bastion or blockhouse.

Caponier - a covered communication across a ditch leading to outworks, usually provided with loop holes. Also a powerful casemated work projecting into or across a ditch to provide flanking fire along the ditch.

Casemate - a bomb-proof vaulted chamber within the ramparts providing an emplacement for a gun and/or a barrack room.

Citadel - a self-contained fortress, usually within a town's fortifications, intended as a defensible place of last resort and for control of the town.

Crenellation - gaps or embrasures enabling the fire of archers or gunners through the parapet.

Cupola - an armoured dome to protect guns, searchlights or observation positions above an underground position.

Curtain wall - a wall around the perimeter of a castle or a fort, often joined to towers or bastions.

Demi-bastion - a work with one face and one flank forming a half-bastion.

Diver - an anti-aircraft defence system against the V1 flying bomb.

Embrasure - an opening in a parapet wall, through which a gun can be fired.

Flank - a side of a work, usually a bastion, between the face and the curtain. The principal defensive element of a bastioned fortification.

Fort - usually a self-contained fortified place.

Fougasse - a drum of inflammable liquid capable of being fired by an explosive charge, usually sited by a roadside.

Horn-work - a detached work beyond the main ditch. The front was made into two demi-bastions on either side of a curtain.

Loop/loophole - a slit or opening for firing a projectile.

Murage - a tax levied for building or repairing the walls of a medieval town.

Muzzle-loader - a gun loaded through the muzzle of the barrel.

Orlit post - a Royal Observer Corps surface observation post introduced during the Cold War.

Outwork - a fortified defensive position in advance of the main defences.

Palisade - an obstacle of close-set pointed wooden stakes.

Pillbox - a concrete or brick strongpoint for small arms or an anti-tank gun, usually part of an infantry defence line.

Predictor - an instrument for predicting the range, height and position of aircraft.

Radar - radio direction-finding and ranging for tracking the approach of aircraft or ships.

Rampart - a bank of earth or construction of stone, brick or concrete, usually with a ditch in front, forming the main defence of a fortress or other defended position.

Ravelin - a triangular, detached work, with or without flanks, set in the ditch in front of a curtain and between two bastions.

Redan - an outwork consisting of two faces forming a salient angle.

Redoubt - a small work in a bastion or ravelin, or, in detached form, an outwork at some distance beyond the main defence. May be in the form of a redan, a square or a polygon.

Retrenchment - an interior work behind the main defence line, to provide defence in depth or to make good a breach.

Revetment - a retaining wall or face to an earthen rampart.

Rotor - an integrated system of air defence introduced in 1949.

Rifled gun - a gun whose barrel has spiral grooves cut in its bore to rotate the projectile when fired.

Smooth-bored gun - a gun with no firing, used to fire roundshot.

Spur - an arrow-shaped projection from the face of a curtain wall.

Stop line - a linear defence, positioned to impede the progress of an army.

Traverse - an earthwork thrown up to prevent enfilade fire along any line of work which is liable to it.

Bibliography

Alexander, C	1999	*Ironside's Line* (Storrington)
Ashworth, C	1990	*Action Stations 9: Military Airfields of the Central and South-East* (Wellingborough)
Bloomfield, P	1987	*Kent and the Napoleonic Wars* (Gloucester)
Bragard, P, Termote, J, & Williams, J	1999	*Walking the Walks* (Kent County Council, the Sydicat Mixte de la Côte d'Opale and the Province of West Flanders)
Brooks, R	1990	*Kent's Airfields Remembered* (Newbury)
Burridge, D	1987	*The Dover Turret* (Rochester)
Burridge, D	1992	*A Guide to the Western Heights Defences, Dover* (Dover)
Burridge, D	1997	*Twentieth Century Defences in Britain: Kent* (CBA)
Clements, W H	1999	*Towers of Strength* (Barnsley)
Coad, J	1990	*Dymchurch Martello Tower* (EH)
Coad, J	1995	*Dover Castle* (London)
Coad, J G, Lewis P N	1982	'The Later Fortifications of Dover', *Post-Medieval Archaeol* 16, 141-200
Collier, B	1960	*The Defence of the United Kingdom* (London)
Colvin, H M (ed)	1963-1982	*The History of the King's Works*, vols 1 and 2 [1963], vol 3 - part 1 [1975], vol 4 - part 2 [1982] (London)
Crowdy, R	undated	*Medway's Island Forts*
Dobinson, C S	1996	*Twentieth Century Fortifications in England* (CBA)
Fleming, P	1984	*Operation Sealion* (London)
Francis, P	1996	*British Military Airfield Architecture* (Yeovil)
Gulvin, K	2000	*The Medway Forts*
Gulvin, K	undated	*The Napoleonic Defences of Rochester and Chatham*
Hamilton-Baillie, J R E	1974	'The Fixed Fortifications of the Sixteenth to Nineteenth Centuries, Illustrated by the Defences of Chatham' *Royal Engineers J* 87
Hogg, I	1974	*Coastal Defences of England and Wales 1856-1956* (Newton Abbot)
Longmate, N	1991	*Island Fortress. The Defence of Great Britain 1603-1945* (London)
Lowry, B	1996	*Twentieth Century Defences in Britain: an Introductory Guide* (York)
MacDougall, P	1980	*The Isle of Grain Defences*
Reed, J	1980	'The Cross Channel Guns', *After the Battle* 29
Rogers, P G	1970	*The Dutch in the Medway* (Oxford)
Saunders, A	1989	*Fortress Britain* (Liphook)
Saunders, A	1997	*Channel Defences* (London)
Scarth, R	1999	*Echoes from the Sky* (Hythe)
Smith, V	1985	'Chatham and London: The Changing Face of English Land Fortification, 1870-1918', *Post Medieval Archaeol* 19
Smith, V	1985	*Defending London's River: The Story of the Thames Forts 1540-1945*
Sutcliffe, S	1972	*Martello Towers* (London)
Turner, H	1971	*Town Defences in England and Wales* (London)
Vive, P A L	1972	*The Royal Military Canal* (London)
Welby, D E	1991	*The History of Archcliffe Fort* (Dover)
Wills, H	1985	*Pillboxes: A Study of UK Defences 1940* (London)